"WALKI𝗡

P

I will always remember where I
October 1989.

I was living in an ex-Keepers cottage in the Scottish Highlands and
I know it was an ex-Keepers cottage because I was the ex-Keeper.

I answered a loud knock at the door to find two Police Officers
standing in the drive. One of them, a young lady, stepped forward
and said they were looking for Brian Carter.

I answered that was me.

She said "I am sorry to have to tell you this, but your father,
Bernard Carter, has died in France"

My knees buckled but I knew she must have it wrong. It can't be my
Dad. He was too young, and it must be a mistake. She must be
confused with Lynn's father who was much older than my Dad and
of quite poor health. I didn't wish that on Lynn but somewhere there
was a mistake.

The Officer repeated it again. This time it really hurt.

She said I had to ring home and asked if there was anyone there
with me. I replied that there was my wife and children. She said
they would leave me to deal with it and they turned to leave. I felt
for her because I think it was her first time breaking such news and
I thanked her as I closed the door.

Lynn had heard everything and was by my side. I told her to pack a bag and I would drive down to the village telephone box and call home. Our telephone had been cut off for none payment of the bill. It was a regular occurrence.

I had to be with my Mum in Yorkshire. I know she needed me, but right then I needed her too.

I had to sort this out.

I didn't know then that my Fathers falling asleep would play a huge part in my awakening. That journey was ahead.

Right now, I had another journey to make to Mum, in Yorkshire.

CHAPTER ONE.

I called Mum.

She was distraught. Her husband and not only left her a widow he had passed in another country.

He had died on the quay in Calais as he was waiting to drive his articulated lorry on to the ferry home. He was lifting some duty-free shopping from a trolley in to the cab when he suddenly grasped his chest and fell to the ground. A British nurse in the car parked next to his lorry saw him fall and was there instantly. There was nothing she could do.

Dad was taken to a mortuary in Calais and the Police informed the company he worked for and they told Mum.

I spoke to my brother Nigel who was closer to Dad as I had moved away from home years ago, and he too was heartbroken. I felt so much pain from down there I just wanted to be there.

The drive to Bradford was a haze. All I know is we got there an hour less than the normal journey time.

I listened as Mum struggled to tell what she knew, and it was clear to us all that we had to get Dad home. Mum, especially, could not accept it until she saw her husband for herself.

Nobody slept that night. I am the eldest son and I just felt I had to sort it out. That's not a slight on my brother. The next morning I rang the company Dad worked for to find out more details. Who I had to call, where Dad was laying and how to get him back. I was totally surprised when they said his wagon was back at the depot already and would I come down and empty it of his personal belongings. The wagon was due out again at lunchtime with a new driver at the wheel.

They weren't being callous. It was a new wagon and the money tied up in one is enormous and the wagons must make money. I said I would get there as soon as I could.

I went alone and was guided to a corner of the yard to where Dads wagon was parked. I was quite proud as I walked towards it because he was a good driver and always had a new wagon. When it had done its time on the Continent, and it was time to hand it down to only make local journeys, there was always a queue of people wanting his wagon.

I opened the door and glanced in the cab and caught sight of his jacket and I broke down. It was a red Toyota Team Europe jacket that I had given him previously. I think I had been holding back but now it was real. I could see his plate and cup in a bowl with the remnants of his last meal. His open case was on the bed behind his seat and his soap bag and towel were next to it.

Somebody came with a few cardboard boxes and I began to fill them with the only things I had left of my Father. I could smell his aftershave from the soap bag in the cab, but I couldn't touch him.

I was given a telephone number of the mortuary where Dad was laying so that we could make a start on bringing him home.

The company Dad worked for were so very kind to us. There had to be a post mortem before they would allow Dad to leave France. It was after all, a sudden death in their country and procedures had to take place. The company offered to pay for the time in the mortuary and the transporting of his body back. Thank you.

I rang the mortuary and they explained what had to happen. They were also very kind too and I came off the phone feeling that Dad was being cared for.

Everything was in limbo. We couldn't get a death certificate until he was back home. Mum called the bank just to let them know and they immediately closed the joint account where their money was kept. She couldn't make any withdrawals. It was just procedure. It would be open again when a death certificate was produced.

We had to wait for the call from France to say he could be released and so we just got on with things. Until that call came we couldn't arrange a funeral date. Mum was in a really bad state and Lynn kept close to her.

I asked Mum where I should put my Dad's belongings. She said to put his case on the spare bed as he always left it there ready for his next trip away. The bed was laid out neatly with new shirts and underwear still in their cellophane packets. Mum and Dad were booked on a cruise to celebrate their 40th wedding anniversary in 3 weeks' time and Mum wanted Dad to look his best. With Mums permission I called the cruise line and cancelled the trip.

I emptied the boxes and was left with his soap bag. Mum said to leave it in the bathroom on top of the toilet basin as that was where he left it between trips. I could smell his aftershave from the bag as I placed it down.

Lynn called the Doctor. Mum wasn't sleeping and was in a bad way. She just wanted her Bernard back home.

We pulled together as families do and we all did our bit to ease Mum's pain, but it didn't. Life had to go on.

When Tuesday arrived I was looking at the Tv channels in the local paper. I noticed that Mark Knopfler and his new band the Notting Hillbillies were on that night at 10:30. I was a big Dire Straits fan and, as a guitar player too, I made a note to watch the programme.

Mum said she was feeling tired and at around 9:00 o'clock she said goodnight and went to bed. It was a relief. We thought the sleeping tablets must have kicked in. Lynn stayed up with me for a while but then too went to bed. I would stay up to watch Mark.

I sat waiting for the programme to come on, but my head was spinning and I too was tired, so not long before the programme started I decided just to go to bed. I set the video.

The house was quiet. I went upstairs to the bathroom to wash my face and clean my teeth. I was drying my face when I smelt Dad. I just smiled and looked at the soap bag and realised I must be smelling his aftershave. No sooner had this thought passed than I felt this overwhelming feeling of Love come over me. It took my breath away with the strength of it and I turned around to see the source of it and I looked straight at my father. I didn't see him with my physical eyes but there was absolutely no doubt he was standing there.

I seized my chance, "Dad I love you, I love you!" and his arms were around me and we hugged each other tightly and he said, "I know you do, I know, and I love you too!" We held each other so tight and I felt a Love that was beyond physical love. It permeated every atom of my body. It was bliss, pure euphoric bliss.

I don't know how long we held each other but there came a point when I knew it was time for him to go. As he stood back from me I felt a sense of panic and I said, "Don't go Dad, don't go, don't leave me!" I felt him starting to rise and I desperately tried to hang on. I was almost lifted off my feet with the immense pull of him leaving. There was a column of light that he was being pulled in to and it slowly faded and disappeared in to the Universe.

I stood in complete awe. I was shaking. The feelings I had were of total bliss and joy of what had just happened.

I went in to the spare room where Lynn was asleep in a single bed. I got in to mine and lay there completely overawed and yet euphoric. I was filled with joy and totally ecstatic. I wanted to wake Lynn and tell her, but she was fast asleep, so I laid there with my heart bursting. I felt Dad again and looked toward the door. He walked towards me and bent down and kissed my forehead. He turned to Lynn and walked over and gently kissed her too. It was wonderful, it was beautiful, and I was full of tears as my heart was breaking.

He slowly returned to the door and looked back at me. I knew this time he was going.

 I called out to him and told him once again that I loved him, and he showered me with a love that once again embraced me. I watched him walk in to Mum's room.

I laid in bed in an absolute gibbering euphoric mess. I really wanted to wake Lynn but what did I tell her? I've just seen my Dad? He came back to visit me? Honestly, he did!

I somehow resisted in waking Lynn and tried to figure out what had just happened. Who was going to believe me? What had, actually happened? What had I seen and felt? Had his Spirit or Soul come back to say goodbye whilst his body was laying in France? I had so many thoughts going around in my head, but I was so blissfully happy.

All I knew was that what I had experienced was none negotiable. It had happened, and it was real, and I was wide awake and not dreaming. I had been standing when it happened, I wasn't asleep. My head was spinning with questions.

I thought about the last time I saw him alive.

He had been up to visit us with Mum in May earlier that year. He loved it up here in Scotland and as we stay quite close to Balmoral Castle they nearly always paid a visit there. He had a humble start in life and he must have been in awe of the grandeur of it. His Dad had drove a horse and cart.

On the Sunday morning that they were due to leave, my Dad was standing in the front garden with his back to me and looking up at the moor in front of the house. The car was packed and ready to go and he was just waiting for Mum. He already had his jacket on. I strode towards him and took a deep breath: I didn't know why, but I just wanted to tell him that I loved him but as I walked towards him he heard me and spun around and asked where the heck was Mum as they needed to set off. The moment was lost.

I must have at some point fallen asleep and I suddenly awoke and leapt out of bed as I heard sounds from below in the kitchen.

I rushed down and flung open the door, dressed only in my underpants, to see Mum with her back to me at the kitchen sink. She turned around and I blurted out "Mum! You're not going to believe what happened last night!" when she quietly said, "I know love, Dad came to me in my dreams and it is going to be alright". I told her my story and although I felt like I was trying to convince her I did see a change in Mum. She was quite calm and seemed serene in some way. She had enjoyed her dream with Dad, but it is too personal to relate here.

We were chatting at the table drinking tea when Lynn walked in. She could sense that something had happened and we both told her our stories. She then told us hers.

When she had left me the previous night to go to bed, she had been going up the stairs when she felt a presence alongside her on the stairs. She wasn't sure what it was but as she said to herself "Don't be worried it's just Dad" she felt a great sense of comfort and a feeling of peace. She was going to come back down to tell me but thought I just wouldn't understand.

My Dad really loved Lynn. She was the daughter he never had, and she then began to tell me in private of a dream she had that night. The undertaker had previously warned Lynn that due to the time delay after death that the coffin would probably come back sealed, especially if a post mortem had to be carried out. Lynn was a Nurse and she understood. He advised us to prepare Mum for the prospect of not seeing Dad again as he thought it would be for the best. We had tried to tell Mum, but she was having none of it. She was going to see her husband for the last time even if it had to be in private and behind closed doors and no matter how much time had passed.

In Lynn's dream she saw Dad laying in the coffin in a blue tunic and he looked so peaceful, and more importantly, he looked fine. He looked just like Dad.

The French authorities were going to carry out a post mortem and then they were not. Finally, they decided to do it and we were given a date for Dad to come home. We spoke to the undertaker about a date for the funeral and the quickest he could do it was the 18th of October. Mum wanted another date as it was mine and Lynn's wedding anniversary but we both said it couldn't have been a better time to say goodbye.

When Dad arrived home, we went to see him. The undertaker took Lynn to one side and said not to worry, it was alright for the coffin to be open.

Lynn took Mums hand and we walked over to see Dad. He looked beautiful and at peace. He was wearing the blue tunic.

The funeral took place on our anniversary. Our two children, Nigel and David, had arrived to say goodbye to Grandad. They were in their late teens and had stayed home until things had been sorted out, and also, to look after our two dogs, Emma and Judy.

My brother Nigel was there with his family too and although he was grieving deeply I cannot presume to tell his story. He was a part of Dad's life when he was back home from abroad and was feeling the loss, perhaps far greater than myself. Nigel had a home life with Dad. Moving away meant I missed out on a lot of family things.

The Church was packed to the brim and people had to stand outside. It was so heart-warming to see the support he had in his final hour. He was a Catholic but wouldn't allow us to be brought up in that faith, and he had his reasons, but Mum, who was Church of England, had decided he had to have a Catholic service.

Nigel and I were Church of England too and the service conducted by the Priest was in Latin. We didn't understand a word but every now and then the Priest would insert Dad's name in the appropriate place and it was then we realised that he was talking about Dad. It angered me that we were saying goodbye and yet didn't understand a word of it. It felt so cold and remote.

At the crematorium the anger was welling up inside of me. It wasn't the Priests fault, he had never met my Dad, but I felt Dad was slipping away from us without any acknowledgement from us.

I decided to say something. I turned to Dads coffin and recited my favourite poem.

 It ends with the words *"Sleep easy child, for God is kind, and speaks softly to everyone"* I had replaced child with father and it felt appropriate.

All of his childhood he had the finger wagged at him and the spoken words of "May God help you!!" It came either from a Priest or his family. He grew up in fear of a vengeful God and could not speak about death in any way. He was taught to fear God and death instead of embracing both.

As I recited the poem whilst looking at the coffin, I finally understood. Dad wasn't in that coffin, it was only the overcoat he wore through this life, and his vengeful God hadn't been vengeful after all. He had been kind as promised and allowed Dad the Grace to complete his journey in this life. He also allowed us our final goodbye.

We stayed with Mum for another few days but by then we had been away for 3 weeks and we had jobs and responsibilities to return to. My brother Nigel and his family would be close to Mum. They got her through some bad days and back in to life.

I returned to Scotland with a heavy heart at leaving Mum behind and a suitcase full of Dads new shirts.

I had said goodbye to the only Hero I have ever had.

CHAPTER TWO.

I started to write this book about 16 years ago. I have been on a spiritual journey that accelerated with my father's passing and I have experienced many more such events. I wanted to share it with the world in a way that would help others to see the bigger picture of life that I was beginning to see. A picture that we are all part of. There are no exceptions, if you choose to seek you will find. You just choose it. In choosing I came face to face with who I am and who I am not and the experience of that was a rocky road for me. It didn't matter, for I knew from within, that there was only one choice to make.

We all have a place on the Tapestry of Life. We know that in 1066 Harold was killed at the Battle of Hastings and as King he will surely have a place on that Tapestry. What about us? What part do we play? Well, we all have an equal part to play, King or otherwise. We don't have to worry if we are worthy of taking part, or what part that is, because the Tapestry of Life can never be complete without each of us placing our piece in to the jigsaw. It is dependent on us to complete it. We are all very much a part of the Whole. If you really choose to be part of the Whole, then you will be.

The question for me was, do I place my jigsaw piece in full awareness of doing so or do I place it whilst asleep. Either way that piece is going to be put in to place. I chose awareness.

I started to write it down. As I wrote I realised the ego was involved. One minute it was ushering me to write and the next minute it was berating me by saying "who would want to read your story??" Who would? I can understand someone wanting to read about Paul McCartney or Winston Churchill or Charles Dickens but a gasfitter from Bradford?

I knew what I had experienced but I didn't know how to express it. I didn't know what I was trying to achieve. I didn't even know where I was going on this journey.

I will try and explain in the best way I can. If I told you that the water coming out of the tap was scalding hot you would know from me telling you that it really was hot. You wouldn't have the experience of it being hot until you tested it yourself and burned your finger. Then from your experience you would have a knowing that it was hot. It looks like knowing something precedes the experience of it. It can also be the other way around. It can also be the experience that creates the Knowing. Sometimes on a Spiritual journey you know something long before you come to experience it. *You just know*. We are being asked to Trust. It's our choice.

I had experienced many things, but it was only by coming to know them, and in a way of knowing that could be explained, that I could write with knowledge. I wasn't at that point. I didn't know what I was trying to say. I abandoned the manuscript.

Last year I tried again.

I had to take more of *me* out of the story and yet still leave enough of me in there for people to know who was trying to tell the story. I want people to know that I have many failings on all levels, that I have let my family and myself down at times, and that I am nothing special. I'm just a guy going about working life and trying to work life out whilst failing most of the time. Again, I stopped writing. I just didn't have the right format to get across the important part which is *the Journey,* without *me* interfering with the writing process.

I'm trying to explain a journey that has led me from seeking the answers from Without me, to seeking the answers Within me. I am trying to show a way, or at least how I tried, to find *home.* To find that peace and divinity that dwells within all of us. That part of us that is the real *us* and that is connected to *All that Is* by way of the Soul.

I wasn't chosen by God to do this. I chose to do it. God doesn't have favourites. We are all born with a soul and the choice to become aware of it or the choice not to. We are given free will and we have a life whichever we choose. That is why we are here, to live the life we have been given, freely and without restraint from God. It couldn't work any other way. We are free to believe or not. Life won't stop if you go through life thinking this is a load of baloney. You can be just as happy and rich and content without having to believe.

Except I couldn't.

I was sent to Sunday School as a child and I was taught about Jesus and his Disciples. He seemed like a decent guy and he had a Father, he was the Father of all of us, and he lived in Heaven. He was called God. The pictures in the picture books showed God on a beautiful white throne with clean white robes and a long grey beard. God seemed alright too.

As a child I just seemed to accept the story of Jesus. It seemed the natural thing to do because it was adults who were telling me and why would I not believe them? I loved the stories about Jesus and his Disciples and the adventures he got up to and the Miracles he performed. Why as a child would I not believe it? Obviously as we grow we can make a personal choice but somehow I never doubted His presence on this earth. What I came to doubt and dislike was the way that religion, and religion of all types, added a fog to the story. It became politics. It became more important to win the argument of which religion was right rather than just see that we are all looking at the same God or Source. We are each looking into our own personal diamond to see the Truth hidden in the centre but we are each looking through different faces of the diamond and the prisms reflect the light in to the centre in their own unique way. We are all seeing the Truth but in a way we can each accept and it brings a unique and divine connection to the Truth. We can agree to disagree about what we see but what we feel is usually common thread. We don't need to kill over it. No religion is worth that. If we seek without the dogma of religion we find our own way without the need to belong in religions that need politics to survive amongst others. I think this may explain why as I developed spiritually I never became involved in large groups of people. I listened, learned and absorbed what I felt was right but I never felt I needed to be a part of a larger circle. The times that I had attended I found there was an instant hierarchy.

Once the conscription of having to go to Sunday school eased, and I could choose, I chose football instead. As a child religious education was not high on my priorities. I wanted to play football for England. My early childhood was mainly in the company of my grandparents who were so loving towards me. Mum and Dad worked full time and so I spent a lot of time with Gran and Grandad and I have truly fond memories of my time with them. Grandad was a great handyman and he could make things out of almost nothing. I remember one Xmas being given my first pushbike and pushing it to the top of the steep cobbled passageway and on to the road. Some of the other kids had been given bikes too and I remember one of the older kids looking at my bike and saying that it wasn't new and that somebody had painted it. I peddled straight home and a bit upset and told my Mum! It turned out they couldn't afford a new bike and so Grandad had fixed up a second hand one and had painted it to look smart. I would never have known if it wasn't for that big kid!

The Sunday school experience had planted a few seeds and piqued my curiosity but there were more important things in my life.

That was how I spent a lot of my life. Curious but not over fussed. As I grew up I experienced other things that were curious too and some were unbelievable co-incidences, but they were just that. Or so it seemed. At that early stage I had no way of telling the signs from the co-incidences.

Life was going on, sometimes good and sometimes bad and a lot of in-between but I was still having a life.

I've realised whilst writing that the point when the curious turned in to a real desire for *knowing* occurred quite some time after Dad had passed. I struggled coming to terms with what I had experienced but that struggle is when the journey moved from my head to my heart and I had to know.

At Dads funeral Mum had organised the local Vicar to say a few words at the wake. Nothing special, just a few words to ease the day and to involve the non-Catholic friends and family.

I wanted to speak to the Vicar to ask questions about what I had experienced. I needed help and understanding because it was the most profound thing in my life up to that point and I needed some insight as to what had occurred. We found a quiet place and I related the story whilst re-living it as I spoke. He listened politely and then produced his Bible. He flicked through the pages and then began to quote verses to me. "Beware of evil Spirits" ....and .." the Devil can come in mysterious ways". I heard the words mouthed but my brain refused to register them. I was in shock. The most beautiful experience of my whole life, the most profound feeling of Love I had ever felt was being quashed as he spoke. I mumbled something in the way of thanks, but I had to get away. Lynn could see I was visibly in shock. I have no ill will towards that Vicar but the door to the Church was firmly closed that day. I had a first-hand experience of God and His wonderful ways and it was being quashed by a religion that would prefer only a third hand knowledge of God and preferably experienced and vetted through them. It seemed that God was really only a story or myth and if you actually said that you had experience of the stories they told about God, and that you had actually experienced God, then you weren't normal in the accepted way.

I received the same reaction from family and friends too but in a much politer way. One friend suggested I had dreamt it all. Hadn't he listened to anything I had said? That hurt. I wanted to share it with other people, but I soon recognised "that look" and gave up.

I had such a beautiful experience when Dad came back to me but I knew I had to keep it to myself if I wanted to have friends. I felt I was holding on to the Crown Jewels but couldn't show anybody which made them and my experience worthless.

I felt very much alone.

It was that aloneness that kept me pursuing the Truth. If I couldn't really speak about it, I could still think about it. That was private time, and nobody needed to know.

CHAPTER THREE.

Although I have said that Dad was my hero, I didn't always feel that way about him.

As a teenager I really resented him. He was extremely strict and the only answer I ever got back when I questioned him why I wasn't allowed to do something was "Because I said so that's why!"

We fought all the time and it drove my Mum and brother Nigel crazy. I had to fight for every inch of freedom. I had to be in at night by a certain time or else I didn't get to go out the next day. It was hard for me because every door I fought to open seemed to automatically open for my brother. Every inch I gained seemed to be a right- of- passage for my brother and most of the times when I got to go out I had to take my little brother with me. He is two and a half years younger than me which is a lifetime when you are 11 or 12. He snitched on me to Mum once when I was a bit older by telling her that I had been in my bedroom with Lynn! He smirked about that for a long time but he was alright as a brother. He still is. If I went fishing with Lynn, I had to take him along too and he somehow always got between us under our big fisherman's umbrella. I have fond memories of our fishing trips together in Topcliffe living on the banks of the Swale under that big umbrella. I think he still goes fishing to this day.

I grew up in Bradford, the wool capital of Britain, and everyone I knew worked in the Mills. If you left school with no qualifications the Mill was waiting for you. We lived in a "back to back" house at the end of Exeter Street next to Grandma and Grandad on Mum's side of the family. This meant that our rear front room wall joined on to the rear front room wall of the people above us and you could hear what was going on! I never knew my father's parents as they had passed before I was born. Living next door to Grandmas was handy because we were latch- key kids. Mum and Dad worked and after school if nobody was in at Grandmas we let ourselves in to our house. It was one downstairs room with a cellar- head kitchen at the back of the room and two small bedrooms upstairs. Mum and Dad had one room and me and Nigel shared the other. There was no bathroom and the only form of heating was one coal fire in the downstairs room. I often laugh when I hear the Billy Connolly sketch about the windows freezing on the inside and being so cold in bed and given a coat to throw over us because there was no extra bedding. Yes, it was true.

Sunday was bath night. The tin bath would come out and a big kettle was boiled on the fire and the bath slowly filled. Dad got in first and then went to the Pub. Mum followed and then the kettle was re-heated and me and Nigel got in. We were told not to splash but there was no chance of that! There were always silverfish earwigs under the rug from the damp. They were horrible!

We had an outside toilet at the bottom of the garden shared by the house at the top of the passageway. Everyone knew that was where the Bogeyman lived. Bowel movements had to be timed well because once you were in bed you weren't going to get out again to go to the toilet in the dark! That was truly the last resort.

For a 5-year-old, going to the toilet in the dark of winter was a harrowing experience. There were no street lights close by and we couldn't afford a torch, but you could easily make out the outline of

Bogeyman the Bog at the bottom of the garden. Going to the toilet in the dark was scary because we knew the Bogeyman was out there. If you made it to the Bog and avoided the Bogeyman it was even worse. If he wasn't out here…...he was in there! With a deep breath I would gently clasp the handle and press down on the latch which made a loud click. He must have heard that surely and sometimes, just as I eased the door open, a voice would shout from within "Bugger off I'm on it!" It was the neighbour from up the passageway, so I had to go back inside until he had finished. That meant another attempt at running the gauntlet from the Bogeyman. The latch would be squeezed slowly again, and I would open the door and walk in to a pitch-black toilet all the time expecting the Bogeyman to grab me.

Once you had finished the terror really began. Everyone knew that when you flushed the overhead cistern it set the Bogeyman free. I had to yank the chain with one hand to flush the cistern whilst grabbing the door handle with the other and then leap outside where he was always waiting. If the neighbour was coming in as you were leaping out, then you had another mess to clear up! I can remember when we moved to 182 Mapperton Rd when I was eleven and we had an inside bathroom. I can remember staring at the toilet, the bath and the light switch in wonderment. We had arrived!

It was also here that I remember my first psychic experience. I would be put to bed by Mum and the light turned out. As I lay in bed with Nigel alongside in the next bed I became aware of eyes staring at me from the dark! It was multiple pairs of eyes that seemed like animal eyes, just as you sometimes see the reflection of a cat's eyes in the headlights of a car. There was no form or substance behind them. It was just eyes and they frightened me. I would call out for Mum who would return and comfort me and tell me I was only dreaming. Nigel wasn't seeing anything so they couldn't really be in the room. As soon as Mum would leave again the eyes would re-appear. She would tell me again that I was only dreaming but as I hadn't fallen asleep since she left the last time I knew in my own way that I was "seeing" them. This went on over a period of time and I never really became comfortable with the experience. I think later I figured out who they belonged to.

Grandma had retired but worked part-time in the Mill at the bottom of Undercliffe St. I used to go down on Saturday mornings around her finishing time and hang around the open door of the weaving shed. Gran would spot me and call me in. No Health and Safety in those days and the noise of the looms was deafening. You couldn't hear at all and so everyone had learned sign language and I would stand next to my Gran and watch her flailing away at the woman across the aisle. It was great!

What was also great was that on the way back home we had to pass the local paper and toy shop. Hey, that wasn't my fault! I almost always had a toy bought for me.

I loved my Grandma and Grandad so much. It felt like Grandma was the only one who loved me and when she cuddled me in to her ample bosom I felt warm and safe. Grandad took me and Nigel all over the place. Dad never had money, time, or perhaps the inclination and so if we got to see anything like the Circus it was Grandad's doing. He took me to watch the wrestling at St. Georges Hall in Bradford where I would scream at the bad guys! He also popped me in to the sidecar on his motorbike and I got to see Trials riding with the famous Lampkin brothers. Nigel was too young then and stayed at home or with Grandma.

Grandma had a son Harry, as well as my Mum, and Uncle Harry married Auntie Anne and emigrated to Canada when I was 5. I remember everyone being sad, but I was happy as Uncle Harry had taken me to the toy shop and bought me a dumper truck as a leaving present! He held one of my hands in his whilst I pulled the truck along with a bit of string with my other hand.

I passed the Eleven plus to go to Grammar school and it looked like life was going to be good for the bright boy in the family. I really think I was the first in a very long line of Carters. When that term finished the school organised a charity event in an empty shop in Otley Rd just at the end of our street. We were to bounce a beach ball for 24 hrs none stop. Dad was away in his wagon so I asked Mum if I could go and she said yes because we had teachers always present with us. We weren't being left alone to run riot. Friday night came, and I turned up at the shop at around six o'clock. My stint arrived and I happily bounced the ball until someone else took over. Around eleven o'clock or so I was bouncing the ball again when I saw my Mum walking towards the shop. She came up to me and said I had to go home. I asked her why, and perhaps for the first time, I heard those immortal words "Because your Dad says so!" I couldn't believe it. I argued with Mum, but she said I had to come right now and stop bouncing the ball. I was hurt and embarrassed because it was in front of all my friends and I had to tell the teachers I had to go home. Dad had come back from the Pub and just decided that he wanted me home. Because he said so.

I couldn't understand why Mum never intervened or stuck up for me. It wasn't Victorian times, it was the 60's. It didn't make any difference because Dad ruled the house. His word was law.

When I was twelve I lied about my age and got a job as a paper boy at the shop Gran used to buy me toys at. You had to be 14 but he didn't seem to care, and I needed the pocket money. I ended up doing two morning paper rounds and one evening paper round. I was still doing them when I left school and started work. I used to work Saturdays too at the fruit and vegetable market in the centre of Bradford. It gave me pocket money.

I persuaded Mum to let me buy a bike from the Clubby book. She could see I had been working hard at the paper rounds and so when Xmas came a joint venture saw the clubby book delivering a brand-new bike. I ripped the big tin mudguards off and fitted a pair of useless, very short aluminium ones and I suddenly had a racer.

I started cycling as a hobby. I soon became bike fit and started to venture further afield than the roads around the house. My aim was to ride to Skipton some 20 miles away. I was soon making it easily on a Sunday and reckoned on the light nights of summer I could make it after school if I rushed the paper round and set straight off. I could be back before curfew.

The freedom the bike gave me was liberating. Getting out and away from home in to the countryside felt like escaping from something. I love the countryside and as I got fitter, I added another 15 miles to the journey by pushing on to Settle at weekends. That was a round trip of 72 miles which at 13 I felt very proud of. I would make a corned beef butty and stash it into my bike bag and eat it along the way. There is a big house on an estate near Coniston

Cold that sits at the head of a lake. At that time there were no trees along the wall alongside the road and you could see the big house about 500 yards away or so. It mesmerised me. I would eat my lunch leaning on the wall and staring at the house wondering who lived there. I fantasised about fishing the big lake every day as the new owner of the house. It still mesmerises me to this day but now the roadside trees block the view.

I joined a cycling club. I was riding with adults and being treated like an adult which added another sense of freedom. I felt like I was being noticed as a person and not an object.

One Sunday, a man who had befriended me, took advantage of my trust and sexually abused me.

I couldn't go home and tell my parents. I didn't have that kind of relationship with them. That was perhaps as much my fault as theirs. I sold my bike the week after and my freedom went with it.

I got over it by doing what the Cancerian in me always does, I retreated to my shell. I dealt with it in my own way and just got on with things. I remember going to school the day after. I came around a corner in the corridor and bumped in to a lad that used to go to the same Club. I hadn't seen him there for a while. We looked at each other and we both knew. Nothing needed to be said. The neon sign above our heads said it all.

When Uncle Harry left for Canada it seemed final. In those days visiting was just not possible. It was a major commitment to raise the money for the fare.

In 1970 Uncle Harry helped pay for a ticket for Grandma and she went across the oceans to visit her son. Grandad had passed, and she was on her own. By now Uncle Harry and Auntie Anne had two children, Christine and Michelle. Gran and our family had seen them both when Uncle Harry had come over for a holiday a few years earlier. Getting to go to Canada was a big thing for Gran and we were all excited for her.

We all missed Gran when she went but it was just a holiday and she would soon be back.

It was the Sunday before Gran came back. At midnight I suddenly awoke and shouted out to my Gran. It woke Lynn next to me and she asked what was wrong. I said I didn't know, I must have been thinking about my Gran or dreaming of her. We soon went back to sleep as it was work in the morning.

I was awakened the next morning by loud and frantic knocking on our front door. I peered out of the window to see Mum standing there. It was 6am. Something wasn't right.

Gran had died the night before. She had Angina, and suddenly without warning, her heart gave way and she left us. It was at the precise moment I had called out her name. Mum was distraught not only at losing her Mum but because she was so far away. I told Mum what had happened when I called out Grans name and we all agreed it was an amazing coincidence.

There was absolutely no possibility of bringing her home in those days, so she was cremated over there in Canada. When she left on that aeroplane I had no idea that I was saying goodbye. It hurt, it hurt like no hurt I had ever experienced before, and I was angry.

Mum arranged a church service to coincide with the one being held in Canada and a local Vicar came around to conduct a service for us. It was another brush with religion on my part.

I told Mum there was no way in hell that I would be there in that room. If that man up there on his throne could take away the only person in this world that I was *totally sure* loved me, then He could get lost. I was hurting but I was angry too with God. This was a different God to the one at Sunday School. This God was cruel and wanted to punish me by taking away the person I could always talk to when I was lost. I was hurting.

The Vicar understood and after the ceremony he came through to the kitchen where I had stayed. He did his best to ease my pain, but it didn't. God had to be punished. I wouldn't talk to Him anymore.

I didn't actively go against God. Something inside of me must have kept the connection alive but it was dormant. I neither promoted God nor denied Him, it was just stalemate. Praying to Him never seemed to generate any results and He only seemed to take things away from me. It seemed to be a one-way relationship.

Losing Gran really did affect me. Fortunately, she had lived long enough for me to have left home and newly got married and so my dependence on her as a confidant was lessened.

It's ok to be angry with God. I didn't realise at the time, but my anger was keeping Him in my life. In holding on to the anger I was also holding on to the cause of that anger.....God.

Sometimes, in those moments of anger or despair with Him or with life in general, we open our hearts and it allows a seed to be sown.

Even in our anger we have acknowledged God. The part of us that believes in Him has prompted us to scream out. It is a way of unconsciously acknowledging His existence, otherwise we may just as well shout at the wall.

The whole world and every religion are aware of "their God". If you stopped a stranger in the street and asked, "have you ever heard the name God mentioned?" I think it would really be unlikely that you came across anyone who said "No, I've never heard that name before".

If you asked the question "Do you believe in God?" you may get a very different reaction and answer. The two questions are deliberately different.

So, we are aware of a God, in some form or other. He is called by many names, but we all know instantly who we are talking about. Believing in a God is personal choice and must always be so.

How do we know that name? How come He has such a big portfolio in the world, but nobody *knows* Him? They only know *about* Him, and that is passed around almost like gossip. It is the same with Jesus. Two thousand years after He visited us we are still talking about it. Jesus gave up his life to deliver a message from his Father to us all. If we just really listen to the Lords Prayer, it contains all we need to know about life and accessing the Kingdom of Heaven here on earth.

.

CHAPTER FOUR

After losing Dad life had to return to normal. There is no other way but to carry on. I had filed away the experience in my spiritual shoebox, a little box in my head where I file things away in my memory banks and save them there until I fully understand them. I don't add to the memory but equally I don't take away. What had happened had happened. It wasn't negotiable.

I had lots of time to think about it in private. I very rarely told anyone anymore except when it became obvious that it was safe to do so with a likeminded individual that would listen without scorn. That was a very rare occasion and always no meaningful answers came out of it.

I was caused to remember an incident that occurred about 15 years before Dad passed. It was Xmas day 1974. It was surreal at the time, but I am always able to remember every detail and after my experience with Dad it seemed to be linked in the same mystery it contained. It could now go in the shoebox with Grandma's coincidence.

We always had Xmas dinner at Mum's. Even Lynn had no objections because it was always a feast and Mum was a good cook. I called my cousin Chris who lived a few miles away and asked him if he wanted to come visit for a while. He agreed, and I set off to fetch him. I never made it.

It was raining hard and I took a bend too fast and lost control of the car. It hit a brick wall on top of a railway embankment and the car came to a sudden stop as it punched a hole through the wall. I left the car via the windscreen and ended up at the bottom of the embankment next to the railway line but not on it.

I sat at the top of the embankment watching Brian laying on the ground. I saw him trying to get up but stumbling. I was just observing, there was no physical or emotional connection, I was simply an observer. I could see Brian had blood all over his face and he was trying to wipe it away to see, and then I saw him trying to climb the embankment towards me. He was struggling a bit but kept coming closer. I watched passively as he got to the top and squeezed past the car on to the pavement. I stood up and moved closer to him as he looked around to gather his bearings. He was looking at a telephone box about 50 yards away and I followed him as he staggered towards it. I had no thoughts, I was simply observing. He made it to the telephone box and opened the door. I moved closer still so that I could see in to the box as the door sprung shut behind him.

He was trying to find loose change in his trouser pockets to put in to the phone box but kept dropping the coins and had to search the floor for them. He dialled a number, but it seemed to be the wrong number and he put the phone down to try again. I just watched. I saw him push the coins in to the box and start to speak. It sounded like he was talking to his father and then he let the phone drop down as he fell to the floor and slumped there.

I started to become closer and closer and then I felt myself spinning at great speed and in a kind of vortex surrounded by a brilliant white light. Then I heard a gentle voice say, "*It is not your time, you have to go back*" and suddenly I was Brian again, but this time I felt the pain of the crash.

An ambulance arrived at the same time as Dad and Lynn and I was taken to hospital very aware of the blue flashing light and the blare of the siren. I asked Dad if I was going to die. He didn't answer and just squeezed my hand. He didn't know the answer because he had just been told by the medic that we might not make it. Brian didn't know the answer to that question either, but his soul did.

I was stitched up and put back together and they did a good job of it. I must thank that Surgeon for his skills at saving my face. To this very day, tiny pieces of glass work their way out of my forehead and leave a tiny pin prick of blood. I can feel it like tiny pieces of grit.

The Voice was right, it wasn't my time to go and I made a full recovery.

Once I was on my feet again I related the story to friends and family, but once again it felt like I was just telling a story and not something that had a profound meaning. The "being out of my body" was very real, but the penny never dropped that it was my Spirit that had left the physical, but was still connected by that invisible divine thread, and therefor had the ability to re-connect with my body. It re-connected simply because, as the Voice said, it was not my time to go.

It was something I just filed away in the shoebox.

The experience with my Dad after his passing had started to make me think.

Hindsight is a wonderful thing. It would be wonderful if we could look in to the future and bring it back to us through hindsight. Then again, maybe it wouldn't. Looking back, I can see what was being shown to me. I was just too blind to See.

For some reason I don't think I have ever had the problem of believing in a Higher Source, a Great Spirit, the Universal Consciousness, a Creator or a God in whatever name you choose. Maybe it was just my childhood innocence and those Sunday school teachings but something inside of me was stirring.

The purpose of this book is not to convince anyone of that Source. I can't do that, it is personal choice. Having said that, you wouldn't be reading a book like this anyway if you weren't curious.

The purpose of this book is to help those already believing, but also feeling they are separate to the Source, or God as the name I choose to use. This book is to help attain oneness of Self and Oneness with All there is. It is meant to help us connect Self to the Soul and become aware of the Souls unity with God. To realise the Holy Trinity within us all.

The problem I have had is in believing myself as being worthy of getting close to that Source, and never ever dreaming of becoming friends with God. I know who I am and what I have done in life, and because I am not perfect, I always felt I didn't have the right of access to such knowledge. However, we can't wait for Perfect, the perfect time and place will never come. We must choose it.

The turning point for being able to write this book, on the third attempt, came when I realised fully, and accepted, that we all have the right to that knowledge because *each of us already has that imbedded in to our soul at birth, and a divine right to access it and to Know.*

The *real* turning point came when I decided to stop fighting Brian and to just *accept* that it is our birth- right to *know*.

That was a huge step. To dare believe that what I knew I knew inside would be revealed to me. It was a tremendously hard step to make and I know it is for anyone who is at that point in their life and just *needs to Know*. Take the step. We don't walk alone.

We need to separate Sainthood from walking a spiritual path.

We are not asked, and have never been asked, to go through life as a Saint or in a saintly manner. Various religions, dogma's, cults and doctrines have taught us that there is a price to pay for our actions. Most tell us that it will come at the end of our life when a punishment will be dealt out. It makes getting to the end of our lives, already knowing how imperfect we are, without committing further mistakes and wrong doings, seem like an impossible task. So, we give up. We think God only wants to talk to perfect people and we know we aren't one, so what is the point?

The point is this.

Saints are not made from perfect people. Saints are made from ordinary people who see their imperfections yet choose to fight on. They know that for them they must keep on keeping on. For those, there is no other choice but to follow their heart.

When we try and walk this path we start to walk in awareness. Not just of our surroundings but the awareness of our Self. Our misdemeanours and our demons' step to the fore. We become acutely aware of them, and it is very easy to be knocked down by them. The ego has a way of reminding us of what a poor specimen we are at times. It is in fear of us at that point. It would much rather have the Being that we are nice and safely under control, and not the Being that we are about to become and of no need of the ego. Stepping free of the ego is not something it wants to allow, and it will fight all the way. Breaking free from its *influence* is the hardest battle we fight and being sensitive and aware is a battle we must win. Trying to live amidst an inner battle is painful.

The punishment we put ourselves through fighting our demons is, I believe, a way of cleansing. It is a way of becoming *aware of who we really are. Of who we are and who we are not.*

Those who are unaware seem to just shrug off their past and carry on with life. It doesn't seem to really hurt or hinder them. When we become aware we find we must deal with all that we are. We can't just shrug it off, but we also can't allow it to freeze us to the spot. We must move forward and the pain of meaningfully dealing with our past is indeed a pain. We are not alone in this for our pain is a beacon of Light that reaches out through the darkness and is seen. The Light doesn't go un-noticed. It attracts more Light towards itself.

In the moments of my own darkness I was given this poem. I would like to share it with you.

"My God"

"There have been some times in my life, when I have bowed my head in shame,

but it was then my Father held me and said "My Son, I share your blame"

And there have been some times in my life, when darkness has come near,

but it was then my Father held me and said "Son, in My arms you will feel no fear"

And there have been some times in my life when I have felt so all alone,

but it was then my Father held me, saying "My Son, I will lead you Home"

And then some times from my heart I'll help someone who's in need,

but then there's only Silence and I cry, "My Father, did you not see my deed?"

And from deep within that Silence I hear my Father's voice.......

"My Son, surely there is no need?

for in the moment of your kindness, it was then, that You became Me"

Kindness not only brings us closer to God but it allows us to come closer to *who we really are* and who we really are is God manifest. It doesn't need to be profound to recognise that. It can be in the simplest of actions.

I have been very much influenced by Native American culture and their way of understanding the Great Mystery. That story will come later, and it had a huge impact of my understanding of Oneness.

They make complicated issues of understanding very simple.

There's an old Indian proverb, which I think is attributed to the Cherokee, and I am sure most of us have read it but here is a reminder.

A Grandfather is talking to his grandson about life. How each one of us has decisions to make along the way and how the outcome of those decisions will affect our reality.

He tells his grandson that each one of Us has a Good wolf and a Bad wolf living inside of us and we listen to each one at different times. There is a battle going on within us.

The grandson thinks for a while and then asks "Grandpa……. which Wolf wins?"

Grandpa pauses and then says, "Whichever one you feed".

That right there, in very simple terms, is the ego. We are caught between the ego and our higher Self. In each waking moment we must choose which part of us to come from. It is a choice, *always,* and if we work hard we can *be aware* of which wolf we choose.

 Don't feed the bad wolf with fear, anger, jealousy, hatred and bigotry but feed the good wolf with all the love, compassion, kindness and laughter we can muster. Slowly and steadily we begin to think about our actions and we stop ourselves, at times, from feeding the bad wolf. It isn't easy, and we make mistakes along the way, but very slowly the good wolf will become fat and the bad wolf will be too weak to influence us. The bad wolf won't ever go away. He is part of Us, but as long as we don't feed him, he will sleep.

We don't enter in to a battle with the bad wolf but enter in to a relationship of making peace with each other. It is accepting all parts of ourselves and not just the parts we like. It can hurt to realise that we aren't the person we think we are but in the accepting of that it opens the door to reconciliation with ourselves. It allows us to deal with the angst within.

CHAPTER FIVE.

My daily life carried on. It had to, but all the time there was a sense of something missing and for a few years I went about life in an unconscious search for my answers.

During the course of my work I was sent to service a gas boiler at a premise. A lady answered my knock on the door with a "You must be the Gasman" and waived me in. I thought she was obviously the owner of the house. I asked if she could show me the way to the gas appliance. She said, "I don't know where it is, where will it be?" I felt like saying well it's your house, you should know! Remembering the customer is always right......I restrained.

Another voice called out from the living room and shouted "It's behind the fire in here" The door lady said "There is someone on the floor in front of the gas fire and she can't be moved just now so you will have to work around her" I looked in to the room and this lady on the floor was about three feet from the gas fire and it left very little room to work. I said, "I think I had better come back another day" but the lady who let me in just said "You will manage". It didn't feel like a request but a command!

The lady on the floor edged herself away from the fire and I had a bit more room. I started to remove the gas fire to get to the boiler behind, and all the while I was listening to a strange conversation. A very strange conversation.

I started to twig that the lady who let me in was "assisting" the owner of the house laying on the floor to ease her back pain. The conversation was flowing and, as I was two feet from both of them,

I could not help but hear every word. It felt surreal but somehow real in that it was meant to be.

I assumed the lady working on the patient was a physiotherapist because the patient was saying things like "oh that feels better" and "I can move now" although when I glanced round the physio wasn't touching her.

At some point the lady on the floor sat up and shuffled out of the way. The physio said she would make a coffee and that "the gasman will have one too". Nice to be asked first but go on then!

I serviced the boiler and was putting it back together and by now the patient was almost doing gymnastics with her sore back! I seemed to be involved but not involved with the conversation but intrigued enough in it to want to ask a question.

I played guitar in a band at weekends, sometimes three nights in a row, and my left hand was cramping up. I had been to the Doctor who gave me pills which eased the pain but as soon as I stopped taking them the cramps came back again.

I found myself asking the physio if she could help my plight and after telling her the story she looked at me and said, "It's because your shoulder has dropped". I looked at her like she was a crazy woman and thinking, "Oh yeah…have you got X-ray eyes or something" but I knew better than to take this lady on!

She said that it was causing a nerve problem in my hand. This was really strange as she hadn't even looked at my hand or shoulder! I still found myself asking her for an appointment to see if she could sort me out. She said "Yes, no problem" so I asked how to get in touch with her. Then she really blew my mind by saying "People just find me". What?! A telephone number would help, even a name, an address and city would help but walking around looking for someone was going to mean knocking on a lot of doors. She eventually scribbled down a phone number and I shoved it in my pocket as I left the house.

When I got home from work, whilst in conversation with Lynn, I brought up the experience earlier. I said that I felt I should go to see this lady. Lynn had a strange look on her face but just said something along the lines of "Yes, if you feel you have to, give her a call". It had been intriguing me all day, so I made the call.

I made an appointment with Irene for the following Monday evening. When Monday arrived I asked Lynn if she wanted to come along. She agreed too readily. We set off on the 30 min drive and arrived on time at a little cottage in the middle of one of the city's best addresses. The cottage was tiny, and a bit run down, and looked a bit lost amongst the splendour around it. It looked a little eerie....

Irene answered the door and ushered us both in to a small side room that was dimly lit by candles and there was a physio's couch in the middle of the room. Soft music was playing. Lynn had that look on her face.

I asked Irene where she wanted me, and she said to lay on the couch face down. I started to remove my shirt ready for the wrestling and grappling that would take place on my shoulder, but Irene said, "You don't need to do that". Lynn had that look on her face and it was becoming a bit smug.

I did as I was told whilst Irene stood along the side of me. I was told to close my eyes and relax. Just as I closed my eyes I saw that look again on Lynn's face but this time she was trying to stifle a grin.

I tried to just relax and was waiting for the onslaught on my shoulder to start but it didn't happen. Instead I felt a heat along my spine and opened one eye to find Irene's hand hovering over my back. She caught me looking and told me to close my eyes and relax. It was another command. I could feel what felt like the heat from a silent hair-dryer on my back. This went on for some time until I was told to turn over. I felt it hard to do so because I felt so zonked! The music was still playing, and I felt so relaxed.

My mind was racing. I was starting to put two and two together and I found myself saying "Irene, I know this sounds silly, but do you believe in God?" She answered very softly "Oh yes my dear, you can't do any of this without God" and I found myself thinking "Do what?"

At that I just seemed to relax. A lovely track started with some beautiful guitar playing that I immediately resonated with. I took a deep breath and as I did so I felt a river of warm energy enter me from the top of my head and slowly work its way down my body. It was beautiful and it made me gasp and as I did so Irene said softly "Just let it happen" and I asked, "How do you know?" and she simply replied she could feel it. It was such a beautiful feeling flowing through me and it felt like all my demons were being cleansed from me. I don't remember how long it lasted but eventually Irene stepped to one side and told me to sit up in my own time whilst she went to make us all a cup of coffee. I started to sit up to be able to talk to Lynn, but I couldn't move. It felt like I had been glued to the table. I cocked an eye at Lynn to see her grinning away and chuckling. Lynn had tippled from our first conversation about it that Irene was a Healer. She had kept quiet so that her rough, tough husband wouldn't be put off and cancel the appointment!

My head was spinning. I had a thousand questions to ask. Irene came back with the coffee and I asked a few of them but I was still zonked. I asked Irene if it was alright for Lynn to *have a go* as if it were a ride on the fairground. Lynn had been suffering from a constantly stiff neck and Irene, after giving me that look, agreed to "give Lynn a go".

I sat in the corner as Lynn lay on the table. Irene barely touched Lynn but her hands were busy all the time but eventually Irene finished and we all sat about chatting. I plucked up the courage to tell Irene about the experience I had with Dad when he passed over. I couldn't believe it when she replied "Oh! What a wonderful experience for you!" *Wow*! For the very first time since it had happened I was talking to someone who not only believed me but was totally happy for me! It felt like freedom. It validated all that had happened and for the first time I didn't feel guilty about talking about it. It just felt so natural to talk about it without waiting for that look that always came.

Irene asked me how my hand was. I had totally forgotten about it but the pain and tingling that had been present when I arrived was now absent! I was told that I would need another treatment in about two weeks and if I wanted to, I should call later and make another appointment. Lynn never suffered from neck problems again.

We left, and on the drive home we had plenty to talk about. What I had experienced I wanted more of. It was beautiful and so far from my comfort zone that I couldn't stop thinking about it. After about 10 days or so I felt the tingling start to come back. It wasn't as bad as before but enough to notice when I played guitar. I called Irene to make the second appointment. By now I had a million questions to ask her because my head was exploding with the experience. I had a second treatment and then I bombarded her with questions. How and why and what! She took it slowly and just said that she was an instrument for the Universal energy to use, it didn't come *from* her but *through* her, and that she was willing to participate. Fine, but I'm an engineer and very practical, so show me the papers and the mechanics of it and I will understand. She just laughed and said I had to let go of that kind of thinking!

I didn't need any more treatment for my hand after that, but I carried on making appointments for spiritual counselling. I needed to know more. Slowly and in her own way Irene began to answer my questions. She explained that what she did wasn't a gift because everyone could do it. I remember protesting something like "yeah, everyone but me" because it felt like something far beyond my understanding and I remember vividly her saying "No, especially you". It was a nice compliment to receive but it was like buying your first pair of running shoes and being told to enter that years Marathon. Yeah right!

Irene was an ordinary person. I mean that as a compliment. She had not long separated from her husband and was renting the house from a friend for her and her daughter to live in. By ordinary I mean that she didn't wear purple leggings and green tunics topped off by a pointy hat. That would have put the male chauvinist in me off. At that time, I couldn't be associating with Pixies!

I learned a lot from Irene that summer. More than I can ever relate. It was life changing for me because she planted seeds that would come to need watering. It was to become my choice to water them or let them die. Thankfully I eventually chose to water them.

Irene didn't stay around long, she had to leave for new pastures. I was lucky in that she recommended I attend meditation classes and gave me a name and an address to go to.

Just before Irene left we had an argument and my arrogance and ignorance soured the relationship. It is something I regret to this day. I don't say that lightly.

Irene changed my life, and for the better, because she was instrumental in changing my curiosity in to a needing to know. That took a few years to bear fruit, but I am eternally grateful to her.

Should you ever by chance get to read this book, please know that you helped me change my life and I am truly sorry for any pain I caused you. Peace.

I called the number I had been given for meditation classes and a lady answered the phone. I was given a place and time and decided to go ahead with it. I was too curious now to let it all fall away and this was my only lifeline.

I arrived at the meditation room oblivious to the meditation already going on and blurted out something like "Hi, how you all doing? My names Brian and I thought I would give it a go!"

Yes, in with both feet, but that's when I met Annette and Anna.

I found meditation almost impossible. I could never visualise the journey that either Annette or Anna would take us on. I could visualise my car needing to be taxed, but the beautiful meadow ahead wasn't in my head at all. That isn't a slight on meditation, but I could not still my mind enough to ever let go. These days I can still myself very quickly but back then it was hard work. That doesn't mean I didn't get anything out of it. Not at all. Occasionally I would relax for that millisecond to allow the patiently waiting Universe to enter my thoughts with an insight or fleeting picture. It was always enough to keep me asking questions of Anna and Annette.

Looking back, I can see that I was slowly beginning to awaken and would *consciously* ask questions of spirituality rather than wait for the next "experience". It seemed, that in a very small way, I was actively seeking and encouraging these answers.

Irene had mentioned that I had a Native American spirit close to me who at times in our conversations, stepped closer. She said he was stepping closer to guide me as I awoke. Irene didn't pass on a name or description just that he was an Indian.

If we are seeking, we must be led to our own answers and not given them. If a teacher tells us our guides name and paints a picture of who they are but we don't *feel it ourselves,* it is a complete waste of time. It is then easy to go around saying "I have an Indian guide called Tall Feather". It means nothing really, it would be like being told the Moon is made of green cheese. It is isn't it?

We must do some work ourselves. We need help and guidance both in human form and from the Universe in whatever way they choose to assist. We need to trust that if we are consciously seeking the answers then they will be given to us. It's not just to *some of us.* It is to *all of us,* but we also must be honest with ourselves. Are we seeking out of curiosity or are we needing to *know? We just need to be honest in which one it is.* Either way is fine. There is no hierarchy on the journey. The *difference* is in what our inner Being can accept at the time and how it will affect us in a physical life. If we are curious, we may be given a series of coincidences to deal with just as I was. How we deal with understanding those is how we will progress. If they are seen as just that, then they will still happen to us, but we have set an awareness level that the Universe can work with. If we choose to take the next step and see that something is happening here, and we had better start paying attention, then the Universe will take the next step with us. It is always *our* choice first. That is hard for us to grasp because it is hard to accept that *we* choose our own progress. We think to progress we need to be given something when instead we have to choose it.

Either way is perfect. There is no hierarchy involved. It is just that we are being given what we have chosen. The Universe doesn't deem that we are only worthy of a certain level. *We do.* That may be a hard pill to swallow if we think we really are seeking but at some level we have chosen it.

Life to me is a circle of birth and re-birth until we choose to not visit here again.

We are each standing on a certain spot on the Circle of Life. A circle has no reference point regarding the "head of the table" so wherever you are standing is the centre of your Universe and is perfect. If you were to look across the circle you may see me directly opposite. I see you too. We are both aware of each other and we both know that where we are standing is exactly the right place in the Universe. *Your* Universe is changing as you seek answers and as they unfold you take another step around the circle. As you look across the circle to smile at me, you have moved, and so when you look directly across at me you suddenly see the Master smiling back at you.

He was standing next to me for a while to help me on my journey. I have taken another step.

Now You are seeing Him, and he smiles across at You.

I now look across at You, but you have taken your step and I now see the Master that was standing next to You and he is smiling because of your progress! The Universe does everything with a smile.

I went to a few workshops with Anna and Annette and it slowly revealed the gentler side of this rough tough Gasman. I had to embrace terms and subjects that were well out of my comfort zone, but I also knew it was the right thing to do. For years I berated that I always seemed to be taught by women, where are the guys in this?! It was actually perfect for my personality. It softened me and revealed a side of me I didn't think I had. I hung around after each meditation and chatted, always seeking answers.

Anna wasn't around too long as she returned to her native Portugal and so I was left with Annette.

I don't know what to say about Annette. I sincerely know that by her leading from the rear she has got me to where I am standing now.

She has been a constant and a rock in my life and I know, absolutely for sure, that no matter what we have spoken about she has never judged me. I never came away from a session with Annette feeling that I had been judged. When you have as much baggage as me to let go of, then coming away feeling un-judged, is a huge compliment I can pay her. It means the door is always open to go back. That is a freedom.

I was becoming more aware of Spirit around me. The tiny pin pricks of light that danced in front of me, the warm feeling of a hug around my shoulders when the spiritual penny would drop as confirmation of my thoughts. Working with Annette was always enlightening. She never told me my answers but led me to them. I would often drive home and whilst sitting at the traffic lights smile at myself as the penny dropped. There will be more about my relationship with Annette as the book unfolds because she got me through a few crisis's in my life.

CHAPTER SIX.

We had planned a holiday in America with Lynn's sister Joan and her husband Peter. We were to fly to Los Angeles for a week and then over to Houston where we would then drive down to Galveston to visit Lynn and Joan's niece Julie and her husband David.

Whilst in the motel in Galveston I picked up a tourist leaflet about the Alabama-Coushatta Indian Tribe living on a small reservation outside of Houston.

We all decided to make a visit. My Native American guide, who I wasn't aware of yet, had maybe piqued my interest. I had no idea what to expect but we followed the signs and drove down a road and eventually came to a building set in some grounds. It contained a store, a small information booth and a bookshelf filled with books in the main entrance. A beautiful young Indian lady informed us that a Dance was about to be performed by the children and would we like to see it? We were delighted and were taken outside to find a dirt circle surrounded by wooden seats, kind of like a small arena. We were in the company of a few more visitors who were already seated.

The dancing was amazing and the singing and drumming that accompanied it touched me. It was simple but primal in the way it moved me. The children did various dances, each representing a native ritual, and their costumes were breath-taking. The beauty and complexity of the costumes is something I can still visualise to this day. The one thing that came across strongly to us all was the sheer joy of those taking part! They were extremely proud to share their heritage with strangers and it was humbling. A small donation bucket was proffered and we all contributed willingly.

As we came back in to the main building I felt like I just wanted to spend some money as a way of just saying thank you for what I had just witnessed. I walked across to the bookshelf and perused the books. They were placed end on with the title written on the spine. I checked through the titles, but nothing made me pick one up.

I entered the shop and had a look around. I didn't know what I was looking for but browsed the shelves anyway. It was mainly items for ladies and children. Lovely jewellery and toy bow and arrows and things like that but nothing that grabbed me. I was a bit disappointed that I wasn't going to spend a few dollars.

I came out of the store and in to the main entrance again. The bookshelf was about 15 feet away. I looked across at it and at head height, face on, was a book in the centre of the shelf. I raced towards the bookshelf and leapt at the book to grab it before anyone else could! There was nobody around. I was alone. I grabbed it without looking at it and held it to my chest. Lynn had come out of the store and had seen me run across and asked what I was doing! I said I'm getting this book, and when she asked me the title, I said I didn't know. I was still holding it tight to my chest and I slowly raised it to read the title.

It was called Black Elk Speaks.

I had no idea who Black Elk was. *I did know however that I had to read this book.* I had leapt across an empty room to get it and I did not know why, but I knew I had to get it before anyone else did. All the other books were still end to end and yet this book had been placed in the centre of the shelf face on. It wasn't there when I looked previously. Strange……

I started to read the book whilst on holiday and I had very strange feelings of Deja-Vou. It felt familiar somehow. It is the story of a Medicine Man, or Shaman, of the Lakota Sioux and it tells of his life from birth in a Tipi through life changing events and the loss of their Native way and life on a reservation. Black Elk was forced to embrace Christianity but realised that the God that was forced on him was the One he knew as the Great Spirit. The difference was that the white man's God was enclosed in a book and a building and whom you would meet when you left this earth. You would almost certainly be punished. He was told that on a daily basis by the Jesuit priests who "taught" him to embrace their God.

 Black Elk's Great Spirit was all around him. The Great Spirit was in everything he saw and touched. The trees grew with the Great Spirit inside them and the streams flowed with the energy of the Great Spirit. Mother Earth beat with the steady beat of a primal drum that touched your soul if you cared to feel it. It was a total living *awareness* of the Creator and Grandfather that he respected in every aspect of his life. I think the term Grandfather Great Spirit is the most beautiful way of picturing the greater force that is within us all. It is almost childlike and in its childlike way it brings simplicity to an understanding of All that Is.

The Native Americans have a saying of "Mitakuye Oyasin". It means *We are All Related*. Just two words that say so much.

It means everything, and everyone, is related. They see the animals, the trees and the people as all being related by the Great Spirit and the life-force that runs through us all. They see it in everyone, not just those who have chosen a religion to follow Home, but in every living thing. It is a Picture of Oneness described in two words. Mitakuye Oyasin. We are All Related.

I read the book on holiday. When I got home I knew that I had to read it again.

I was sitting outside of a house in my van waiting for a customer to arrive home and I had the book with me. I had about 15 minutes to wait and so I started reading it again. A very warm and loving feeling came over me as I started to read. It felt firstly that I was not alone, and secondly, that I had been in the land that I was reading about. It was as if I was remembering things that I knew. I can't explain better than it was like reading a play that I knew I had been in but couldn't remember the script. Just a wonderful feeling of familiarity.

I kept feeling a wonderful presence around me as I continued to read. Not overpowering to stop me in my tracks, but a gentle feeling of someone close by. I tried to connect consciously but as I did so I just pushed it away. I was new to this. My experiences with Spirit previously just seemed to happen, but I was now starting to consciously try and bring them towards me.

I went to see Annette to tell her of my progress. By this time, I was probably visiting about every couple of months or so and we would have a catch up on my progress. I told her about Black Elk and how I was feeling someone close to me. Annette took me in to the quiet and I sat there just contemplating it all. Suddenly I felt that warm feeling again only this time it was much stronger, and the feeling grew rapidly. Although I couldn't see with physical eyes I knew Black Elk was standing in front of me. His energy was beautiful, and I knew he was the Indian that Irene had seen and was now revealing himself to me. Now I *felt* it, now it was *real*, and I knew for myself his name. It had all come from my own inner feelings and wasn't just passed on by someone else. It really was real.

His presence in my life encouraged me to read other books about the Native way of living and understanding. It was such a simple way. It removed all barriers of colour and creed and just brought us all together as One nation. They couldn't see a separation, but it was eventually forced on to them as their land was divided and fenced to enforce a separation.

It is not for me in this book to cast judgement on how they were treated and where they are left now in this world, but there are many books written that show a systematic removal of the Indian from their lands. Children were removed from their families and sent to state Catholic schools to be taught a good Christian life and have the Indian removed from them. Whilst the authorities had perhaps good intent in turning them in to American citizens it is very sad that those who were perhaps the closest to the Creator had their voice silenced by persecution. They were aware of a Creator in all things around them, but now He was contained in a book and a building.

One night I was lying awake and I became aware of Black Elk. Lynn was sleeping, and I was laying on my left side facing the wall. The wall seemed to dissolve and I saw Black Elk standing there with a log cabin behind him in the distance. He was at a younger age than in the book, I would say around my age, and he was holding across his chest a Chanunpa, the Peace Pipe. He was wearing what looked like a dark blue cottoned shirt which surprised me as I suppose I was expecting to see him in ceremonial garb, or dare I say it, looking like an Indian. He looked at me with kind eyes but with barely any expression as his arms reached out to me to offer the Pipe. I looked back at him, but I couldn't bring myself to accept it. He retracted the Pipe and again it was held across his chest. My mind was spinning, and I was unsure of what to do, but just then he offered the Pipe once again with his arms outstretched to me. I didn't move to accept it and again he withdrew it. I was now in a panic. I knew I wanted to accept it but just thought I was not worthy. I looked again at his kind face and he stepped forward and offered the Pipe once again. I was frightened I had lost the moment and so this time I reached out and took it from him. He smiled gently and stepped back again and slowly faded away. *Wow!* I was once again feeling that spiritual euphoria and I woke Lynn to tell her. It was truly a very special moment for me on this journey and I cherished what I had received. *I didn't know what it meant.* I assumed it was just Spirit acknowledging my journey in a symbolic way and as I was really studying the native way of seeing things, what better way to do it. I felt proud but humble at the same time.

I had been reading a lot about their culture and wanted to experience it myself. With Lynn and a few friends, we booked an RV for three weeks and flew in to Denver in mid-March the following year.

We collected the vehicle in Denver and me, Lynn, Susan, Vince and little Cara then drove up to South Dakota to visit Pineridge Indian reservation. It was an eventful trip, never having driven anything so big on the wrong side of the road in a different country, and there were mishaps on the way! We never got arrested but it did come close with one over zealous Cop in Deadwood but that's another story.

We arrived early on the Sunday morning in Pineridge and decided to visit the cemetery on the hill. I need to say at this point that all through my journey Lynn has been on a similar journey. We both felt the same way about the Native Americans and Lynn had recently found out she too had an Indian guide by the name of Red Cloud. Vince and Cara were also at the awakening stage, so it was ideal for all of us. I have to say that Cara has since become a fearless warrior for spirituality and I like to think that some of the seeds were sown on this holiday.

It is worth digressing at this point to explain something I have found to be true. When you are searching from the heart and involve yourself with Spirit then you *feel* the truth. Our emotions are very strong, and they show us through a feeling of *knowing* that what we are *feeling* is real. It is like sharing a common truth. I have a nephew Jake, a great little guitar player and all round decent young man, and when he visits us from Yorkshire to the North of Scotland where we live, we always have some deep conversations. He asks the right questions. I explain the best I can but tell him he must only take away from my answers that which he *feels* to be true. He *should* question. What he doesn't *feel* right now, may or may not become apparent to him until later, but it is Jake's journey and not mine. I take him for a walk in the woods surrounding our house which is my sacred space. I show him how to feel the energy from the trees and when he does *feel* it I know because I am shown the same energy at the same time. I can tell by his face he is feeling it, but I also *know* he is feeling it. I told him of two trees that form a gateway at the top of a path we would walk down. They are about 12 feet apart and there is a "gate" between them. I told him we would go and feel the gate. I knew the outcome already, but I could see he saw it as a test! He asked what if he didn't feel it, what if he failed the test of feeling it. Would that make him unaware? I told him it wasn't a test and was only a walk through the trees and to relax. When we got near to the two trees I told him we were there and to walk forward until he felt the gate. I could see he was worried about failure, but he stepped forward and stopped at the right spot. His face lit up and at the same time I was shown the energy he was feeling. He *knew* he was feeling it and so did I. It showed me he is becoming aware. It showed Jake too. He simply felt the energy each tree gives out constantly and he met in the middle and felt the universal energy that is all around us.

We entered the cemetery and walked amongst the graves. Although it may be a sad place the beauty of them is heart-warming. They are adorned with flags on each corner of the grave in the colours of the Four Directions. They are decorated with feathers, personal possessions and fabric that proudly shows off their relative that is lying there. We walked on and came across Chief Red Clouds grave. Lynn had a special moment in private there. She came away knowing he wasn't there. He was everywhere the wind blew and in every direction. It gave her solace and peace. I had looked for Black Elk's grave but couldn't find it and I was a bit disappointed.

We walked out of the cemetery to a couple of benches not far away. The sun was shining and we all wore shorts and T-shirts despite it being March. We just sat basking in the sun and contemplating what we were feeling about the place. An old Indian sauntered over and nodded and motioned to the spare seat next to me. I gestured for him to sit down. He did so and asked if that was our RV parked there. I said it was. He then said to make sure we were bunkered down on a site by 6 o'clock as it was going to snow and there would be a storm. He then got up and walked away.

The others had heard it too and we all chuckled as he walked away. We were toasting in the heat. He was just a kindly old Indian and we didn't know what to make of it. We were soon to learn respect.

Whilst sitting there a younger Indian came over and sat with us. He introduced himself as one of the many great-grandsons of Chief Red Cloud (name withheld) and we all got talking. He said he had seen us from the Diner and that he felt he had to come over and talk to us. It was kind of surreal that we were meeting a relative of a Chief, but it also felt good. I asked him where Black Elk was buried, and he didn't seem to know which puzzled me. Black Elk was a famous Indian from this locality and I expected him to know. He thought it was over Manderson way, which was just past Wounded Knee. We were just about to get up to leave to go there, when he said he would like for him and his brothers to do something for us. He said to come back to the Diner in a couple of days and he would have something sorted out. He also said he just needed some money for tobacco to have as part of the ceremony. Hmm. Alarm bells were ringing as we had been warned we would meet those who said they were members of famous Indian families and if we just donated a little money……. We gave him some money and hoped we would see him again.

We set off through the reservation to Porcupine and Wounded Knee. It is worth pointing out that Pineridge reservation is a very poor county. It is unsettling to see how they have been abandoned by most of the USA. We arrived at the scene of Wounded Knee Massacre. It *was* a massacre and not a battle. There is no other way to describe it. Even the USA government has made an apology. We did the usual tourist thing and read the Historic marker and looked around the Church and the graveyard. It was hard for us to imagine what happened that New Year's Eve in the snow, but the story is very sad. We could feel the sadness and the cemetery there is a reminder of what took place. I can still picture some of the graves to this day. I later wrote a song about it. We drove on up the road and in the direction of Manderson. We didn't realise it but we had passed the turn off to the cemetery as we drove along. We eventually came across a battered old sign at the end of a dirt driveway saying Black Elk museum. Woahhhh! We had to visit there!

We drove down the dirt road to arrive at a few log cabins and a few barking dogs. Our arrival was kind of obvious! We looked around for a Museum but couldn't see anything resembling such a building. One of the cabin doors opened and a young lady asked us if she could help us. We told her we were looking for the Museum, but she said it wasn't built yet. An old lady then appeared at the door of the same cabin and introduced herself as Olivia. She said she was trying to get a museum built in memory of her grandfather Black Elk. We were actually talking to a living relative of someone who was so close to me! She invited us all in. I was trembling.

It was a nice warm cabin, very simple but welcoming. Off to one side was a room where the young lady who had come out to see us was working with another lady in the manufacture of Native American quilts. Olivia explained that the family wanted to raise funds to build a small museum in memory of her grandfather and father. Her father was Ben Black Elk and he was the son of (Nicholas) Black Elk and was responsible for interpreting the Lakota language in to English to enable *Black Elk Speaks* to be written. Olivia was a lovely warm and welcoming lady, the kind you would love as a Grandma, and she talked with us willingly. The girls had a look at the quilts in progress and Lynn asked if she could order one. Olivia looked chuffed! She pulled out some coloured squares and asked Lynn about the colours she would like. Lynn said she would leave it up to Olivia and I saw Olivia giving Lynn *that* look. She then announced "Ok, I got it!" I plucked up the courage in a private moment to tell her that her Grandfather was helping me from Spirit and she reached out and squeezed my hand. It was a very special moment. To her it was natural that her ancestors were still helping in this world. I was too taken in by the wonder of it that I relented in telling Olivia about the gift of the Pipe from her Grandfather. Although I didn't know it then, that would come later. Her family are very naturally protective of her and after around 30 mins or so a couple came in from the cabin across the yard and asked how we were getting on. They said that Olivia gets tired and not to stay over long. They were smiling but we took it as a sign to leave. Before we left I asked Olivia where her Grandfather was buried. Olivia told us that whilst Black Elk was alive he had never been made a Chief but in death the Tribe had honoured him with that title and we would see it on his headstone. She was very proud of it. She gave us directions to the cemetery and we said our goodbyes.

We collected the quilt a year later and it adorns our bed. What a lovely reminder.

The cemetery was on the side of a hill on the right as we drove back to Manderson. We parked outside the gate and entered the cemetery. It was just a very simple graveyard on the side of a windswept hillside but once again the graves were decorated with flags and coloured tape and there were the graves of young children with toys and other personal belongings. To see a small grave so beautifully decorated somehow lifted the sadness.

I wondered around on my own looking for Black Elk's grave. Chief Red Cloud had a monument at the head of his grave and so I looked for something similar towering above the spot but none of the graves had anything like that.

I eventually came across a headstone with the words Chief Black Elk chiselled very simply in to the stone. Just a simple stone of remembrance. I sat by the grave and talked to him. I knew he was free from the body that lay there but it still hurt sitting there. I found myself crying. Here lies the man that was changing my life and it just seemed so poignant to be so close to him and his last resting place.

In the ensuing years Black Elk taught me so much about Oneness and how we are all a part of the Great Spirit. If you see things from Black Elk's perspective it is hard to wilfully destroy anything, for anything you destroy also destroys a part of yourself. If they needed timber to construct a Tipi or to burn on a fire they always gave thanks to the tree and to the Great Spirit for providing their needs. It is a very simple way of acknowledging that the tree is a part of the Whole and is being recognised as such. In a crowded room don't we all like to feel someone acknowledge us?

Black Elk taught me so many concepts and one of them was the concept of letting go. One evening I was home alone and sitting in my chair in the stillness. I meditate with my eyes open but not focusing on anything in the room. I had an awareness of another Spirit that was helping me, but it seemed to be from afar. I was contemplating on it and beginning to wonder who was guiding me besides Black Elk. I sat for a few minutes dwelling on it and then finally asked *Who is my guide?* At that moment I began to be aware of Black Elk stepping forward and I felt comforted in some way and I simply voiced *"Oh, so it is You"* and with that he simply stepped aside and raised his arm and pointed far and wide. At that moment I felt an energy coming towards me that was like a Tsunami wave in its width and depth and the energy was so strong that my body began vibrating and I was lifted from my seat. It was the most powerful energy I had experienced up to that point and it left me a gibbering mess. I was deliriously happy but I couldn't seem to operate as a human being. It took almost a week to come back to normal energy levels. It was Black Elk's way of saying that the Universe is our guide and that we shouldn't limit our source of knowledge to one being. I came to trust Black Elk totally. His energy is serine and calm and he emanates the truth. I began to be too comfortable and dependant that he was there and so I was taught how to *let go.*

I was leaving the house one evening and was just about to set off in the car when I became aware of Black Elk close to me. He seemed to be saying goodbye and I almost went in to shock with the realisation. He was leaving me after teaching me so much and I needed him close. I was shaking at the thought of him leaving and felt I would be on my own and I didn't feel ready for that. He faded away and I had to drive off to my destination. The following days and weeks seemed to be very bland and I was finding it hard. I finally decided to focus on what he had shown me when the tidal wave from the Universe visited me that evening and I started to move on. One day, whilst alone I finally said goodbye to Black Elk and thanked him for his guidance through spirit and through the books he caused to come my way. I was extremely sad and tearful, but I stood up knowing I had said my farewell. I walked a few steps and became very aware of his presence close by. I turned to find him smiling at me with that beautiful serene smile and in that moment I accepted the concept of letting go. I wasn't letting go of Black Elk, I was *letting go of the need* for Black Elk. It taught me a lesson that has helped me so much through my life.

After saying goodbye at the graveside, we left to drive through Wounded Knee again and began heading out towards Rosebud reservation which would be our furthest west before we would turn and come back through Pineridge again and visit the Badlands.

It was 5:45 pm when the first snowflake hit the windscreen. By 6 o'clock we were in a blizzard! I mean a real, full on, blizzard. We made it to Rosebud late that night and there was a car park outside of a Diner and so we just parked up and bedded down. It was too late to look for a site. The next morning we ate at the Diner and we all got our first taste of Indian fried bread. A kind of greasy pancake. By the end of the holiday we were loving it!

The weather had caught us out, and so we had a quick look around before deciding what to do. There wasn't an RV site open in Rosebud at that time of year and so it was going to be camping by the road in this weather. We had passed a sign for an RV park as we left Pineridge and so we decided to head back there. Not long after heading back and not far out of Rosebud we came across a store (name withheld) at the side of the road selling Native American memorabilia. It is now closed. We pulled in and entered the store. It was mesmerising. There were wonderful items of clothing beautifully decorated with Sioux beading and lots of bracelets, hats and jewellery. The craftsmanship was amazing. An Indian man came from the back and introduced himself as Harold. A white lady soon followed, and Harold introduced her as his wife. I have withheld names out of courtesy. They were used to seeing tourists coming in who were sometimes aware and interested in their culture and they chatted to us freely. They made us coffee and made us feel very welcome. It felt very easy to talk to both of them and we felt relaxed in their company.

I took Harold to one side and asked if it was possible to be able to see a famous Shaman in the area who had written a couple of books. Harold just simply said it might be possible, but he will just take your money. He will just see you as a $50 bill. It was a real shock. I had been wanting to talk to a real Indian about the significance of the Pipe, so I opened the conversation gently. He took a sideways look at me (I'm getting to know it now) and said maybe he could help. Now I'm sorry to say this, but I was a bit disappointed in that he was just an ordinary Indian. Forgive my ignorance, but I am just being honest and if not a little unaware and rude too. He motioned to a back room and pulled out two chairs and placed them facing each other about six feet apart. He said fire away and so I told him about the visit from Black Elk. I was nervous because here was a white man telling an Indian that another Indian, and a famous one at that, had given him the sacred Pipe. I expected scorn or a rage at my disclosure, but he just listened quietly. When I had finished there was a long pause. This is it I thought, here comes the wrath. He looked across at me with *that* look and caught me by surprise when he asked why I took the Pipe on the third time of offering. I said I took it then out of panic because I knew I wouldn't get a fourth chance. He told me that you must never accept it on the first or second offering but only on the third. I could not have known that at the time, but something had made me hold off from accepting it the first two times of offering. I felt that energy within me that I was getting used to by now telling me that I wasn't alone and what I had just heard was the truth. He asked me if I knew what Carrying the Pipe meant. I said I didn't, but I would like to know. He went on to explain that not everyone accepted it because it was a responsibility to the people to be on call when needed, to give up a certain lifestyle, and that at some point in life the Carrier would be called on to stand up and be counted for the People. He said that not everybody wanted that responsibility. I told him that at the time I had received the Pipe that I had been willing to carry it. It seemed to come natural to me at the time as part of the gift. He shook his head and smiled and said something like "Oh well! There ya go, wait and see what comes of it". I had a fleeting moment of doubt.

We learned a lot in the store about how Indians lived in modern-day life. A lot of the teenage girls would make jewellery and bracelets from porcupine quills and beading woven together. It was very intricate, very colourful and very beautiful even to a guy. It helped them pay their way through college. A lot of the kids were coming out of college and training to be Lawyers and Doctors. It was fascinating learning about the modern Indian. Harold asked where we were staying and after discussing the severity of the weather he offered for us to stay outside the store and to hook up there. It was a very kind gesture.

He then said that he wanted to take myself and Vince in to the Sweat Lodge!

 Oh Wow! This was something I had read about, dreamed of taking part in, and here we were about to experience it with a real Indian!! I can only speak for myself, but I was trembling because to me it was a very, very special ceremony to share. I knew from his reaction that Vince was excited too. Harold said he had things to prepare but he would be back the next morning. We all chatted about it well in to the night. I was about to experience a dream come true.

The next morning Harold returned to the store to take us to his house. We followed Harold through the snow to his house on the banks of the White River. It was a nice but simple house situated on its own and surrounded by prairie and the rapidly flowing river close by. Snow was deep on the ground and it was absolutely freezing.

The Sweat Lodge was as I expected it to be. A fairly small dome covered with blankets, skins and anything else that would both make it light and water tight. There was a flap at the front facing the east for an entrance. Harold had gathered twigs and brush in the firepit to one side of the Lodge to heat the rocks we would take inside. We helped with gathering wood for the fire and Harold explained what would happen. In short, we would enter the Lodge with a good heart and we would pray to the Great Spirit for help and guidance. We would do four rounds of prayers, each round followed by a few ladles of water on the hot rocks to create the breath of the Great Spirit to ensure we were heard and that we spoke the truth. The fire was soon roaring fiercely and the rocks were ready. Harold carried them in to the pit in the centre of the Lodge along with a small bucket of water and a ladle. We removed our clothes and stood in the snow naked and waiting. He was ready.

The Sweat Lodge is a sacred space. I knew it was to Harold and both myself and Vince knew it was to us too. Our intent was pure. It wasn't a game of curiosity. I can only relate what happened in general terms for it involves other people, but I can tell you what I personally experienced.

Harold poured water on to the red-hot rocks that were glowing in the dark and it really *was* dark in there. The steam rose quickly and we could feel the heat building up. Once he had created Grandfathers breath with the steam, he said a prayer on our behalf and on behalf of his own people. It was sincere and heartfelt. He then added more water and created more steam and then Vince and myself said our own prayers out loud in turn. After each prayer was voiced more water was added and the heat and spiritual intensity grew stronger. By the time we had said the fourth prayer the heat was almost unbearable. It was so hot that I thought I wouldn't be able to endure it to the end. Then again, nothing would have got me out of there until the ceremony was completed.

After the fourth round we all went quiet and in to the stillness to allow Grandfather to talk to us should He wish to. I was sweating beyond sweating. Hot water was running down my face in to my eyes and I was so wet my hands couldn't clear it. The heat was intense but so was the spiritual energy. I felt the left side of my face burning and then becoming dry. As I noticed the increase in energy around me I realised a Wolf was licking at my face and drying it. It wasn't frightening at all, but it *was* absolutely mesmerising. My hands were so wet that I couldn't feel if the side of my face was dry but I knew that it was. This lasted for some time and the Wolf then lay next to me. I was crying and joyful at the same time. It was such a beautiful experience and I felt truly blessed. When Harold said the final prayer, we knew it was time to leave and he opened the flap which I think came as a relief to both myself and Vince.

I stepped out naked in to the snow and gasped fresh cold air in to my lungs. I felt my face and knew then it really was dry on my left cheek where the wolf had licked me whilst the rest of me was dripping in sweat. I quickly said to Harold "look at my cheek, it's bone dry!" and then told him about the Wolf. He just smiled and said "Ugh, Ugh". I asked him what it meant but he just said that it was for me to find out. It was a tough answer but it was the one I needed. We were told that normally we would leap in to the White River and cleanse ourselves in the cold water but the river was raging with water from the snow and it was not possible. We threw snow at each other instead! We had gone from unbearable heat to being frozen in minutes.

The girls had kindly been allowed to shower in the house and the three of us also had showers.

We had coffee and fried bread and a really enlightening conversation with Harold and his wife. They are beautiful people.

Whenever I sleep alone at home the Wolf often climbs on to the bed. The bed actually moves, and I can feel his physical weight on the bed and I can feel the covers tighten as he lays beside me. There hasn't been any conversation yet, but I know I am safe and protected and I cherish his presence. It is still happening today.

We said our goodbyes and headed back to the RV site at Pineridge. It was closed. The Indian lady owner said that the electric had been cut off and there was no water in the shower block, but we could stay there if we wanted to for free, and to just go ahead and pick a slot. We gladly accepted although we didn't take it for free as it was obvious to us that they were experiencing difficult times. That night the temperature dropped to -32 degrees and with the wind chill it went down to -43. It was intensely cold in that RV that night! We had connected the water hose to fill the van from the stand pipe and there was a small spray of water as it filled. Once it was filled that spray and the connecting pipe had frozen and the following morning we had to try and remove the hose through two feet of ice with only plastic knives and spoons. I remember Vince throwing a hot cup of water in to the air and it freezing in to snow before it hit the ground. It was cold!

The next day we were to meet young Red Cloud at the Diner. With some difficulty we managed to extricate the van and headed to the Diner where we would eat warm and desperately needed food. We sat around waiting, drinking more coffee and waiting and waiting. It became obvious to all of us that nobody was going to show up. We decided to head off through the Badlands to Rapid City.

We filled up with fuel and were just pulling away from the pump when a pickup truck pulled across the front of us and skidded to a halt and blocking our exit. It was young Red Cloud and two other people. He leapt out and said he had been looking for us and had tried looking in the RV site but we had left. He told us to follow him. We followed him out in to the prairie down barely visible and passable snow-clad dirt roads before we came to a sheltered spot in amongst some trees. We parked up and they came in to the RV to join us. We were introduced to his cousin and friend. We asked if they wanted anything to eat and the friend laughed and said, "Let me tell you, never ask an Indian if he wants food because the answer is always Yes!" and so we gave them food and coffee and started to talk. We started to understand how poor it was on the reservation; how difficult life was because there was no industry. The only place of work was the Casino which then took back the wages that were earned through the tables. Alcohol was a big problem. Once we had all stopped talking they said they wanted to sing for us.

I can remember not knowing what to expect but they started singing in Lakota and in harmony and accompanied themselves with small drums. It was beautiful, very primal but very intense and it didn't just fill your ears it filled the air and your body with a sense of not being separate from it but being part of it. I can still see the wonderful depth in the eyes of the younger cousin, like deep pools that drew you in to the wonderment of the Universe they contained. It was a very simple performance but it was filled with wonder, joy and peace. We each took something special away with us.

It was getting late and we wanted to see the Badlands in daylight and so we postponed the journey and went back to the RV site.

The lady saw us arrive and told us that young Red Cloud had been looking for us. He had been telling the truth.

The next day saw us setting off for Rapid City through the Badlands. It is a bleak and desperate place even in summer and yet that bleakness is also beautiful. We drove through the hills mesmerised by the sheer wildness of it. The Indians used it as a hiding place from the white man in times of trouble and you could see why. You could disappear in there very easily and very quickly.

Somewhere in the middle of the Badlands we came across a very old and battered sign that was hand painted with the scrawl "Coffee and food 3 miles ahead". We thought it would be a good idea to stop if it was open. We turned off at the next sign and down a bumpy track and eventually came in to a yard. There was a broken-down building with smoke coming from the chimney and a few other dilapidated sheds but no sign of a coffee house. We thought we were in the wrong place and we started to turn the RV around when the door opened and out came a couple. They asked if they could help but we said sorry to have bothered them, but we were looking for a coffee house and we seemed to have taken the wrong road. They said we had the right place, but they weren't open until spring. We apologised and started to move away when they asked us if we needed food. We told them that we were ok for supplies but had just stopped to break the journey. They beckoned us in and wouldn't take no for an answer.

We were ushered in to a large warm kitchen with a big bare wooden table and a log fed stove in the corner. We took a seat all the time saying we didn't want to put them to any trouble. It was no trouble. The coffee pot was put on the stove and a large frying pan was placed there too and filled with bacon and fried bread. The interior was very basic and it was obvious they just got by. We ate and drank and talked. The lady made her own jewellery and asked the girls if they wanted to take a look. I think out of politeness they agreed but the lady produced some truly wonderful samples of her work and they were soon trying on bracelets and necklaces. The lady supplied them to the stores and the price she offered them to us was so below what the stores charge that it felt like you were stealing them. The man of the house made Indian flutes and Vince sampled a few until he settled on one he liked. A price was agreed and Vince became the proud owner of a genuine handmade Indian flute. They were great hosts and again told us about the modern ways and how they just managed to survive. They didn't have an easy life.

The time came for us to leave and they walked out to the RV with us to say goodbye. We said something to them, which I can't remember, but it was along the lines of thanking them for sharing their food with us and for helping us on our journey. I will always remember his reply *"No, I have to thank you guys. It's been a long winter and we won't make anything until spring. That was the last of our bacon but thanks to you guys we now have enough money to buy in a few supplies to get us through until May. We are so grateful to you for stopping by"*. It was amazing. They had given us the last of their bacon, and, long before the conversation had opened up to jewellery and goods for sale. They had just given freely without motive. It is times like those that stay with you. What a memory to treasure.

We reached Rapid City that night and found an RV site with electricity, water and hot showers. We needed all of those.

CHAPTER SEVEN.

Although the RV site was quiet it did have all the facilities open. After finding a site we all showered and changed to go in to Rapid City to eat. We found a Taxi firm number on an information board and called a cab.

The driver chatted away and then out of the blue, announced that they were a grandchild of Black Elk. It hit all of us like a brick to the head. The driver then went on to say that we were supposed to meet and that we needed to spend some time together over the next few days to learn more about the Indian way. It seemed incredible to us but we wanted to know more and so we agreed to go along with it.

As we were dropped off at a large Country and Western line-dancing Club that also did meals, our heads were spinning! We all thought what an amazing co-incidence and we were all excited.

One of the nice memories of that evening was meeting the live band that were playing to the line-dancing audience. I went to the bar to order drinks for us just as the band took their break and a couple of them came up to the bar. I expressed my compliments to them and said they sounded great and that we were all enjoying the band and the dancing. I explained that I was a guitar player in a band back home and that Vince the keyboard player was also on holiday with us and as I did so Vince came over and we all had a chat about the usual musician geeky stuff!

We returned to our table and shortly afterwards the band came back on stage. The singer/bass player switched the PA back on and suddenly announced to everyone "Ladies and gentlemen......we have a couple of guys in the audience that are all the way from Scotland and they play in a band together... will you please put your hands together for Vince and Brian!"

WHAT?!

They motioned us up to the stage and we both looked at each other in shock! The audience started clapping and cheering and we found ourselves being coaxed to the stage. There was a big problem looming here, we didn't know *any* line-dancing songs! We scrambled onto the stage and the guitar player handed me his Stratocaster guitar whilst asking quietly what songs we knew. We said that the only country song we played in our set was Take it Easy by the Eagles and the singer/bass player said they knew it. Vince took his place in front of the keyboards as the keyboard player stepped back and I slung the guitar strap over my shoulder as the drummer counted in! Talk about being put on the spot!

It was fantastic! Vince can sing harmonies and he accompanied the singer whilst the keyboard player stepped up to the singer's mic and also added harmonies and it sounded great. When the song came to an end the audience cried out for more but there was no more! We quickly explained that the kind of stuff we did was rockier and as an example I said, "things like the Stones and Alright Now by Free" and then the bass player started playing that familiar bass riff that comes just before the guitar solo in Alright Now. The drummer counted in and we were off again! Vince and I couldn't wipe the smiles off our faces as we played and watched the audience dancing in formation to the most unlikely of songs! When it came to the guitar solo the bass player fluffed the bass part that introduces it but I came in to the solo on time and we finished the song. The bass player was a bit annoyed that he had fluffed his part and ran through that part again…...the drummer kicked in…... and we were off again!

I will never forget that night. The most unlikely of scenarios and yet so thrilling and enjoyable. Apart from a couple of festivals it was probably the biggest gig we had done!

We called the cab number again for a ride back and the same driver appeared. We chatted, and by now we were all very intrigued about what had been said. We arranged to meet the next day and went for a coffee and a chat. We were excited meeting someone so connected to Black Elk and someone who was going to help us on our journey. We found ourselves inviting this person over to stay with us in Scotland at a later date in order to carry on with the teaching. We took a few days to tour the area and we visited the monumental task of carving the statue of Crazy Horse in to the side of a mountain. It is a spectacular site to visit. Although the RV site had full facilities the weather was really bad, and it was well below freezing every night and even leaving the heating running didn't stem the cold. We all decided that it was just too difficult and impractical to carry on staying where we were, in deep snow, for another 12 days or so of our holiday. Having decided to head south to Arizona where the temperatures were in the 70's we concluded our relationship with the Taxi driver by exchanging phone numbers with each other. I had spoken about my experiences with Black Elk and I guess I was singled out as being the one to focus on. We said our goodbyes and headed south the next day. I am deliberately playing down this encounter as the reason will come later.

It was a very long drive down to Arizona and we took turns to drive through the night so that we didn't have to stop except for food and fuel. We drove through the beautiful Arches National Park and Monument Valley on the way and it really is a wonderful and spectacular place to visit. Some fantastic scenery and some fabulous memories to cherish. We eventually arrived in Sedona and spent a week there in the lovely sunshine. It is a beautiful place, especially once out of the town, but it felt like it was geared to "buy your spirituality here" and I think you need to look a bit deeper than the shop fronts to, perhaps, find something deeper. Maybe it has changed over the years but that's the feeling I took home with me.

The holiday came to an end and we headed back up to Denver and the long flight back home. It was a fantastic holiday with lots of great memories and lots of things to think about. It is probably the best holiday I have had.

About a couple of months or so after getting back from our holiday we arranged for our friend to come over from America and stay with us.

We gave this person free reign of our house and the use of a car when needed. Unfortunately, we found out this person wasn't who they said they were and was not being truthful on any level. I arranged for a couple of workshops for them to have a voice and suddenly what was supposed to be a free workshop had to have a charge to attend. It was "an exchange of energy" and I allowed it to go ahead. There were so many other signs that my ego chose to ignore.

After about a week or so it became clear that something was wrong, and I was feeling uncomfortable about it all. One day whilst I was washing the dishes at the sink, a comment was made by this person about my Father. It was something that I was supposed to have said about him, but it was so untrue, especially about someone so close to me, that I spun around to confront this person.

I just saw darkness sitting there.

I told Lynn and wasn't too surprised that she too felt the same way. The next day I went to work and thought about nothing else but our situation. We had brought this person over and so it was our responsibility. I confronted this "friend" about it and the outcome of our discussion was that they were welcome to stay the rest of the holiday. They could freely use the car and the house but there would be no more teaching. It would just be a holiday from now on.

The next evening we heard a clatter on the stairs to see this person coming down with a suitcase in their hand and everything packed. We asked what was happening and were told that they were going to stay elsewhere for the rest of the holiday. At one of the workshops they had met a lady who ran a store in the city and they had called her to say that they had been thrown out of the house. A car pulled up and off they both went. It was very insulting to our hospitality, but another opportunity and person had arisen for this person to take advantage of.

I don't want to dwell on this whole episode and that's why my text is curt, but a lot of things were said that were just not true. My friends were fed lies and told that I was a fraud and that I wasn't seeking real answers and so this person was leaving. If you are a white man seeking a way to the truth through Native American spirituality and the Indian "teaching" you renounce you as a fraud, then it has an impact on all those around you. It is just human nature.

A lot of mud was thrown and some of the mud stuck. To this day I know that some people still hold on to what had been said. It was painful to go through. It almost stopped me believing in myself and I nearly gave up the search for what I was searching for, especially as I didn't know then what it was that I was truly seeking. This episode really threw me and I lost all self-confidence, and I again did what I always do, I retired to my shell.

It didn't just affect me. It affected everyone that had become involved with this person who was coming to "show us the way". A lot of people were let down by it all. I felt very responsible for their trauma too.

Life must go on and it did, but I had lost a lot of the drive that was pushing me to fill the void inside of me. It felt like something had been snatched away from me and as usual I punished myself for causing it to happen. In reality, it was only me that was holding myself back. I should have believed in myself more and carried on, but I was hurting so much that I couldn't see it that way. We never can.

About three or so years after this episode I received a call one night. It was the lady who had taken this person in and it was a call right out of the blue and unexpected. I had tried to have a conversation with this lady at the time about how this person was behaving but of course I wasn't believed, and I had felt the chill in the conversation as I tried to explain. This time the lady was telling me how I had been right all along and that she had been conned out of money and goods. I don't know if it had been preying on her mind but the call she made to me gave me a lot of solace and comfort. She felt she had to let me know. It eased the pain a little and I thanked her for taking the trouble to call.

CHAPTER EIGHT.

It wasn't very long after that I started drinking. It wasn't due to what had happened previously, but my own weakness. I had become a manager at work with a company car and had a decent salary but I was empty inside. I have a self-destruct button that, even in times of success, if I get a little too close to being happy, I press the button. It's even worse if I am at a low as it is so much easier to press that button.

I began coming home later and later at night after work because everyone knows that you can hide behind alcohol. Until the next day that is. If you wish to continue hiding you have to call at the Pub on the way home and it soon becomes necessary. It soon becomes a way of life and if you have a wife at home waiting for you then you soon destroy that person and your marriage, or at least in my case.

Lynn asked me to leave. It was as simple as that. It had been going on for about six months or so and I wasn't the same person anymore. I didn't want to talk about home life or any problems we were facing, and she just had enough. I could see what I was doing to our marriage, but I couldn't stop it. The big Red button was keeping my hands firmly pressed on it. We agreed that I would leave and a friend kindly asked his mother to let me rent a spare room. She took in the occasional lodger and the room was vacant and so I had somewhere warm and safe to stay. It's funny how quickly you come to your senses. I have never been dependent on alcohol, but I have enjoyed its effects on me. I enjoyed drinking socially and having a laugh with the band or with friends, but this was different. I didn't *need* to have a drink, but I did need to hide behind it. I had to take control of my life again and so I stopped drinking.

We were still talking to each other. It was a bit frosty on Lynn's part, but I expected that. I gave her space but it was hurting. We have known each other since we were fourteen and were a couple at fifteen. We were married at seventeen and although life wasn't easy for us, we somehow managed to get through it.

It's easy for any of us to look back in hindsight but Lynn was the real rock in my life. I let her down on many occasions and yet she hung on when she should have just walked away. This time she had enough, and I didn't blame her. She deserved better.

We had to speak on the phone over family things and eventually I felt a softening in her voice. She asked me what I was doing about my washing. She knew I had to have a clean shirt every day for work and suggested that I come around to the house on Sunday mornings and use the washer and dryer. She wouldn't be there, but I had a key and could let myself in. I remember the first Sunday arriving there and seeing her car wasn't in the drive. My heart sank. I let myself in to the empty house and did my chores, all the time hoping Lynn would arrive back. She didn't.

This happened a couple of times. The washing got done but there was no sign of Lynn. It gave me time to reflect on everything I had thrown away and the pain was real. I had chosen it. I had given Lynn no choice.

It must have been around the fourth or fifth week that I was just leaving the house with my washing in a bag when Lynn pulled in to the drive. We exchanged pleasantries, but she didn't invite me back in. I must admit driving away after seeing her was heart-breaking.

I can't remember why, but Lynn phoned to ask me to call around on the Wednesday night. I built up my hopes that maybe she wanted to talk. When I got there it was to discuss a family matter and then the conversation stopped. It wasn't about us. I was empty and emotionally drained. I tried to engage her in a conversation about us, but she wasn't ready to talk and her resolve that it was over was firm.

It was a warm summer evening and we had talked in the front garden. We lived in a beautiful cottage with freedom from neighbours and at the foot of a hill in the distance that I used to work on when we first moved there. Lynn was digging amongst the shrubs and I decided to just leave her in peace and take a walk up through the fields to the start of the moor. I told her where I was going, and she acknowledged it and as I set off I saw her kneeling on the ground attending to some weeding with her trowel.

I walked through familiar fields up towards the moor with my head filled with thoughts that I had finally blown it. There was no going back, and I had got what I deserved. It wasn't a sorry for myself conversation I was having with myself, it was just a fact. You can only stretch a bond so far until it breaks, and I had done all the stretching it could take.

At the end of the fields there is a gate. If you go through the gate you are heading out to the moor. It is a road I knew so well from working on the hill and I had travelled it hundreds of times in the past. It was getting a bit late to go through the gate and reach the lunch hut further along the road, and so I just leaned on the gate and reflected on my life. As I began to feel the depths of my situation I just started to cry. I was alone with nobody within miles and I just let it all out. It wasn't self-pity, but it *was* a realisation of what I had caused and what I had lost. I just sobbed until I could sob no more. I felt totally drained and resigned myself to a future without Lynn.

I'm not sure how long I leaned on that gate, but it came time to turn around and leave. I set off to walk back to the cottage and collect my car from the driveway. I was totally empty inside and felt so alone.

I must have walked about a hundred yards or so when I felt a presence on my left side. It was a very safe and warm presence and it got stronger as I walked.

I felt the presence grow in intensity and I was aware of being spoken to in my left ear but I didn't know what was being said. I just knew that it was happening to me and as I relaxed a little I was lifted off the ground by an unseen Being. I seemed to float about 2 feet above the ground and all the time being aware of a conversation going on that wasn't verbal and given in a way that I didn't understand except to know it was happening. I can remember vividly looking around to see if anyone was around who could see me floating above the ground as I walked forward but of course there was nobody there. It was surreal but real. I knew I was being carried along by an unknown presence that I felt safe with. It was truly an amazing experience and again I am not sure how long it lasted but eventually I became aware of being lowered back to the ground. When my feet hit the ground I just stood there in awe and immediately there was a huge flash of light within me. It was like the flash of a camera and lasted just as long.

I started to walk forward again but this time *I knew what I had to do*. I didn't have an answer in the form of any words but I just "knew" what I had to do to resolve my situation. It was another out of body experience similar to when I had the car crash. My physical body was obviously walking on the ground, but my Spirit had risen to communicate with the presence carrying me. Once I regained my body my Spirit knew the information that was inside of me but I couldn't remember it.

I reached the cottage to find Lynn still on her knees in the front garden. I so wanted to tell her what had just happened, but her head was down amongst the flowers and I knew it wasn't the right moment. I ended up just saying goodbye and I got in the car and drove away with Lynn with her head still down in the shrubs.

Later that week I received a call from Lynn. She said that if I came again on Sunday to do my washing she would be in and she would make a bit of lunch. My heart leapt with joy, but I told myself not to build up any hopes. It was natural that a couple who had been together for so long should be able to act civilly towards each other and it would be nothing more than that. I arrived with my bag of washing and Lynn took it from me and put it in the washer. I hadn't been expecting that and it was a nice touch. We chatted whilst it was being done but it wasn't really about us but at least it was conversation. We had lunch and it was time for me to go. I can remember not lingering on and making the moment harder for either of us and so I just said thanks for lunch and drove away. The following Sunday was approaching, and I hadn't heard from

Lynn and my heart was sinking. I arrived at the cottage to find her car in the drive and my heart jumped. Again, we had lunch and this time the conversation was much softer. I drove away feeling much less alone.

I received a call from Lynn mid-week saying that she wouldn't be there on the Sunday morning if I went around but if I wanted to leave it until later she would be back late afternoon and "perhaps I might want to make a curry" for tea? Oh yes! I wanted to make that curry.

We talked about us. We talked about trust and everything that goes with it and slowly but surely we became friends again. One Sunday Lynn asked me if I wanted to come back home. I returned to the flat and brought all my belongings back home. I told Lynn what had happened to me on the hill and that I somehow knew on that night what I had to do and she understood. Lynn was far more aware than I was.

I was still playing in the band with Graeme, Vince, Iain and myself. When I had been apart from Lynn we still had gigs to do and it kept me going. We were a very popular band and we had bookings almost two years in advance. It was a double-edged sword. On the one hand you knew you were popular enough to be booked ahead but you also knew exactly where you had to be in a years' time. It applied to all the band members and not just me and we found we had to sit down at the beginning of the year and sort out our individual holidays so that we could please our families and the band. It wasn't easy! Often, I would be asked to attend something or be invited away for the weekend, but I would look at my diary and know we were booked. It wasn't easy for any of our families either and at times caused some friction.

The band was freedom for me. It was an escape from reality being on stage playing guitar. It was as if it wasn't me playing but my alter ego and I could embrace the music and forget my woes. It was filling the void that still existed within me. We played almost every Friday and Saturday nights with barely a weekend going by without playing. Every third Sunday of the month we also did a gig at a Pub quite local to me. It wasn't too bad because being a Sunday they closed at 11pm and if I was quick enough packing up my gear I could be home by 12:30 instead of 3;00 am if it was a Saturday night. It was, after all, work in the morning. Most of my work colleagues returned to work on Monday refreshed after the weekend whereas I was always worn out.

The following summer we played at the same Pub one Sunday evening. Lynn said she would come down later as she knew some of the wives and girlfriends would be there and she could have a catch up. About half way through the gig Lynn appeared and sat with them and enjoyed their company.

I was tired after the gig and so I packed up my gear as soon as we had finished and said my goodnights and left Lynn to carry on chatting. She would follow home in her own car later.

When I got home I went straight to bed. We had played three times that weekend and I had to work the following day. I knew I wouldn't be able to sleep knowing Lynn would be back soon and so I picked up a guitar magazine and started to read. I was absorbed in the text when I felt a presence coming from my left side and near the door. The feeling grew stronger and there was so much energy and love in the room that I found myself looking over at the door to see if I could see the source of all this beautiful energy.

All I can say is that my eyes were drawn to the doorway and as I began to sense the source, very slowly and deliberately, an Angel started to manifest in front of me. As my eyes raised upwards from the sandaled clad feet, the body of the Angel became solid at the same speed my eyes were slowly being drawn upwards. It was as if I could only raise my view slowly and as I did so I was totally mesmerised by this magnificent Being in front of me. When my eyes locked with the eyes of the Angel, I saw my face. It was an androgynous version of my face, neither male or female but unmistakably my face. The face was so serine and benign and emanating a sense of peace and calm. The light being emitted from the Angel was as bright as a powerful strobe light but without the flashing as it was just pure Light. The Angel's breast and torso were covered with the whitest of feathers that glowed with a pearlescent sheen that flickered gently and shimmered in the light. Whiter than the whitest swan you have ever seen. My eyes were drawn higher and I could see the enormous and beautiful wings towering above the shoulders. They towered way above the door and brushed through the ceiling in a wonderful and powerful arc. I was totally mesmerised. It wasn't a "flicker of light" or a "sense of Spirit" it was solid and real as a real person. I had no fear because all I was feeling was very safe and very loved. I was being loved totally, through every fibre of my body which was trembling with the energy. In the right hand the Angel was holding a sword that was held like a cane with the tip of the sword touching the ground and it was tucked tight in to the side of the Angel. It wasn't menacing, it was just what it was, a sword held in a peaceful and non-threatening way.

The Angel simply stood there, fully manifested and solid, as in not being able to see through, for quite a time. I have no idea how long, but it was long enough to take everything in. No words were spoken, nothing seemed to be transferred to me except an amazing feeling of love, peace, serenity and safety. A great sense of "everything is as it should be" and then slowly the vision faded away and I was left dumbfounded. I felt wonderful and mesmerised at the same time. It was beyond anything I had experienced before because when I had seen Spirit previously it was always in a form of energy, but you just *knew* what you were seeing. This was different. The Angel was solid and, up to that point, the most beautiful experience of my life. I was shaking with joy.

Lynn arrived back home and I told her all about it. She could see I was shaking with wonder and the joy of it all and we both basked in the experience. She was genuinely pleased for me. I didn't sleep that night. How could I when my head was filled with wonderment and awe.

I was going to call in sick from work the next day because all I could think about was the Angel, but I knew it wasn't the right thing to do. I went in to work thinking that I would whizz through my jobs and get away home early where I could just bask in the experience freely within my own thoughts. I wasn't functioning too well, especially as an engineer. I couldn't believe it when I was given a day's work 20 miles away from my usual patch and one of the worst jobs we ever had to handle. It was to re-gasket a 25-year-old boiler that was leaking water and it was the very last job I wanted.

My protests went unheard and I drove away from the depot feeling fed up knowing it would be a late finish.

I got to the job and emptied the central heating system so that I could pull the sides off the boiler to replace the rubber gaskets. The bolts always break as they are rotted with rust, and sure enough, the very first bolt snapped. It means having to drill them out and re-tap the holes to take new bolts, a very long job with 16 bolts on each side. Inside I was cursing. I had gone from absolute sheer bliss to instant reality within twelve hours.

The next bolt came undone and I whispered a silent thanks to whoever may be listening and then the third bolt came out, and the fourth, and the fifth. My mood started to lighten up and I couldn't believe it as each bolt came out in one piece and leaving a thread to be able to fit a new bolt in to. I got the job done in record time and all I wanted to do was to get away to be free to think about the Angel that was running through my head. I really wasn't functioning too well on a human level either.

The job was in the next village to where Annette lived and all the while I had been doing the job, I had been thinking that I had to tell Annette because I knew she was the only other person I could tell. I drove the 5 miles and knocked on Annette's front door.

She took one look at me and I will never forget the words she spoke on the doorstep: *"Hmm…that big eh?"*.

Yes, it was that big. I thank God that Annette came in to my life. Having someone so aware and so normal was needed in my life and she has been with me in support with every step I have taken on this journey and yet I know I have driven her crazy at times by not seeing the wood for the trees. I hope I am making amends.

This may seem incredible to anyone reading this, but it took many years for me to realise that it was my Guardian Angel I had seen. An Angel that was with me through any of my incarnations as either male or female and through any event in my life. An Angel that was with me every step of the way. Sometimes I am very slow at grasping things. Wood for the trees comes in to mind again.

I settled down, accepting what I had seen but not really understanding it. The questions came and kept on coming. Why me? Why not someone worthy? What is it telling me? What did I miss? What do I do about it? I didn't have answers to any of them. Not one.

A few days later I went to bed and fell in to a deep sleep. I had a very vivid dream, the kind you can remember when you awake.

I was standing alone at a gate that leads to the moor. As I turned to walk away an Angel flew alongside me. Slowly one of her wings wrapped gently around me and she lifted me gently to her side and whispered in my ear as she carried me along the road. She was speaking to me softly in my left ear and as she finished she eased me slowly and gently to the ground and stepped back to watch me. There was a blinding flash and the Angel smiled and gently withdrew knowing I had accepted her healing.

CHAPTER NINE.

As usual, life went on. It went on in the usual unconscious way it had always done. My spiritual shoebox was slowly filling with wonderment and fantastic experiences but I just couldn't tie them in to my real life. There was that separation from the experience and my actual life. I was very aware of what I had experienced, and I knew that everyone didn't have these experiences, because if they did, I would be able to talk openly about them.

The time came to leave the band. It had run its course for me and I knew it was time to walk away after a gig we did one New Year's Eve. We played that night to a packed crowd who were going to celebrate the New Year with a bang! We played well and had encore after encore and it was after 2:00am when we walked off the stage.

I remember vividly, the exact moment and the exact spot on the roundabout when I just said to myself "time to go". I was driving home around 3:30am and was reflecting on the night. We had played really well, but when we had taken a break after the first set and retired to a small bar away from the crowd, we sat at two different tables. The band had split in to two camps. It wasn't anybody's fault, it was just the way of it. It was just life, but it felt awkward.

The next morning, I awoke knowing I had made my mind up and I called Graeme and said I was leaving. I would give them as long as they needed to find someone else, but I was leaving. I think it was a relief for them too. They found another Brian to replace me and this guy really could play guitar!

It left another void in my life, a big one. My diary told me where they were playing each weekend and I always found myself thinking about it knowing they were on stage and without me. It was my choice. It had been the best band I had ever been in and I missed it and them. It had been my choice to leave and I took that on board.

The following year, exactly to the day, we had a knock on our door on New Year's Day morning. We lived in the middle of nowhere, so we weren't used to visitors. It was a couple of Shiatsu and Yoga friends that Lynn knew and we welcomed them in. We chatted, and I put an album of relaxation music on in the background. I had told them I had left the band and didn't want to join another as it was so tying and that although I was enjoying the freedom, I was missing playing.

A track came on that I really loved. It was the very same track that came on in Irene's house when I went for healing. I had purchased the album after hearing it at Irene's. It has some great guitar playing and at the very exact moment it started I was asked what I was going to be doing musically in the future. I replied that I would love to do "something like this" and as the words came out, I felt that spiritual warm shiver run through my body. They saw it too and one of them said "If that isn't a sign, I don't know what is!"

It left me wondering if that was even possible. It mulled around in my mind and the type of music suited the way my life was going. I often sat quiet, not quite being able to lose myself in meditation, but just chilling. It didn't matter about the meditation because I remember Annette saying to me "I wouldn't worry about that, you are a walking meditation anyway". I think that was some sort of a compliment or perhaps that I was not quite here, or it could be there. She may well have meant I wasn't the full shilling.

I was well known in the local music store that was run by a couple of friends, Ross and Bill and the staff knew me too. I used to help for free on some Saturdays just for the fun and the experience of it. There were two young lads that worked there that had been working with a local female singer and had some success in meeting record companies and producers and were getting a little studio together. I approached them about the project, telling them that I wanted to tell a story through music and they seemed keen. They kept asking me when I wanted to start but I kept putting it off. When I had really thought about it more, it just seemed something way beyond my talents. Adam, however, wouldn't let it go and kept pushing me. I found myself going in to the studio with Adam and Simon "just to discuss it". No pressure, and just for a chat. I told them the story I wanted to unravel through music. The beginning of our planet, life emerging and the animal kingdom arriving followed by man and it all blending and coming together, to Walk in Harmony, which became the title of the album.

We sat and drank tea as I explained what I wanted to achieve. I remember being asked how it started and I just said, "with a bang!". Adam got up and went to the desk and fiddled around with a drum machine and a reverb effect and created a "bang". We worked on the sound to make it very faint and in the distance as if it occurred very far away in the Universe and we were off! We created an even quieter bang that followed the initial one and sounded even more in the distance and it created a sense of time.

Adam and Simon are very talented musicians that rate way above my own talents and it was quite intimidating at first. I found myself out of my depth and comfort zone and having to make it up on the spot. That's what great musicians do, they create music out of thin air but unfortunately, I'm not one of them.

After the "bang" came turmoil until the planet finally settled down and peace took over the earth and life on our planet began. How do you describe that in music? Well, we created wind and rain and deep "growing pain" sounds from within the earth's core by using a synthesiser and sound samples. As the planet settled down water began to run and out of the water the plants began to grow. How do you make a plant grow in music? By Adam playing the most delicate, sparse and beautiful piano. Very gentle at first, but slowly building in intensity to simulate growth and that day I came away with 4 minutes of music on a cassette player! We had started. No going back now. No chance of me making excuses anymore it was real and happening. I had to knuckle down and get it finished.

I put every part of my heart and soul in to creating that album. Adam and Simon did too. I might not be the greatest musician, but I became the catalyst to it becoming a reality. I created the story and between us we created an album. It stretched me in a way that I had never experienced before. I would have to come up with a guitar part and a melody that fit the story and play it over the chords I had given Adam for the keyboards. I would be awake at 2:00am working on my parts knowing I was in the studio the next day at 11:00am to record them. I would fall asleep knowing I wasn't yet ready but the next day I would somehow manage to get it down. It is one part of my life where I really *knew* I was being helped by a source greater than me. Some of the parts I played did come out of thin air and when I listened back to them, I realised they *weren't played by Me*.

I didn't realise it as I was writing, but I had written the two halves in one key but using the major key for the beginning of the album and the minor key for the ending. When it came time to complete the last track and combine the animal kingdom and the kingdom of man together to form the title track, Walking in Harmony, the two tracks overlapped and fitted together perfectly! What a strange co-incidence.....

It took some time to create the album but finally I had it in my hand. I had paid for it with money and by trading guitars, but the reality was I had a finished album in my hands. Simon and I decided to have it mastered at Air Studios in Cambridge, so we booked time there and went down to have it professionally mastered. We sat with the engineer as he played each section and adjusted the levels and the EQ so that every sound could be heard in balance. Simon watched every move the engineer made and as we left, he said, "I know how to do that now". That's talent, and it came in handy for the next 6 albums we were to make. If somebody had said to me at the time that I had another 6 albums to make I would have run a mile. One had just about finished me off!

I knew I had to get the album out. The biggest label at the time for that genre of music was New World Music. I didn't want to just send it off with a covering letter and so I got in my car and drove all the way down to Norfolk and handed it in at the reception. A lovely lady named Diane, who was then the office manager, came out of her office to take it from me. I told her that all I wanted was for someone to listen to it and not put it in a pile. The outcome didn't seem to bother me as long as it was heard. That would be the test of the strength of the music. Diane assured me it would. I got in the car and drove straight back home, a total trip of 26 hours. It was now out of my hands.

A couple of weeks later I got a call from Diane. They were going to release the album, and could I come back down to Norfolk to sort out a deal. Wow!

I went down to discuss it but being a new artist to the label they wouldn't sell it on a royalty basis. They would only buy the album from me as a one-off payment. I argued but I didn't get anywhere. I spoke with a few other labels, but they were the same, they just wanted to buy it outright and the price they offered was lower than the one made by New World. I signed with New World Music and the artwork was sorted out via email and the album was released. It went to number one in their own charts for 3 months and sold well. It got great reviews from new age critics.

I once walked in to a house to service a gas boiler not long after the release. I saw on the coffee table a New World Music brochure and on the front of it was my album! I was so excited but I didn't say anything. Appearing on the cover of a music catalogue whilst servicing a boiler seemed worlds very far apart. I just smiled all day. For me personally, it was a huge achievement.

I released two more albums with New World but both on a royalty basis with an advance on sales. The second album was "the Heart of the Circle" and was written about the stone circles that were all in close vicinity of the house. Each circle gave off a unique energy and as I picked up on that it was easy to create a musical story. I enjoyed making that album much more than the first! It wasn't easy, but it *was* easier.

The third album was a follow up to Walking in Harmony called Living in Harmony. It was the second of what was to be a trilogy. The premise is that if you start to *walk* in harmony with yourself you would start *living* in harmony with yourself. This would eventually bring peace within yourself and so the third album is to be Peace in Harmony. It turned out to be quite prophetic. I haven't written Peace in Harmony yet and perhaps I never will, but I am at peace with myself. It's hard for me to write that. Maybe it's the right time to start making music again.

In 2016 I was on a flight from the UK to Australia via Dubai and as I flicked through the in-flight entertainment, I had a wonderful surprise. In the chill- out music section was Walking in Harmony. I didn't listen to it, and I never told John my travelling companion, but I did have a huge grin on my face for the rest of the flight!

Simon had continued to help and perform on the two albums after Walking in Harmony and it just seemed right to form a duo and give him the credits he deserved. We formed Gentlethunder and proceeded to record together. It came from a name I was given earlier that summed up my character perfectly! New World Music didn't want me to "dilute" the product they had created with my name on it by adding Simon and so I asked that I be free to record under the name Gentlethunder and they allowed me that freedom. Actually, they couldn't prevent it, but I thought it was polite to ask.

I then made a big mistake. The music industry is the same one-sided business regardless of what genre you record in. Just because you record from the heart with an intention of imbibing your music with good vibes doesn't mean it will be seen that way by a record company. You are just a product. I released it with another company and it was a disaster. I soon realised that the company I was dealing with was nothing like their public face. It shocked me after everything I had believed. It was time to pull out before it was too late. I won't go in to details, but we were both glad to be free.

There's a saying about the music business: *The music business is a cruel and shallow money trench, a long plastic hallway where thieves and pimps run free, and good men die like dogs. There's also a negative side.*

The partnership with Simon under Gentlethunder did spawn two more albums we are both proud of. It usually starts, but not always, by me coming up with a storyline. If I can create a story and relate it to Simon, he is very receptive to it. He feels it and that is his way in to the story. We then work together to produce the tracks to create an album. We made *Echoes of the Spirit* and followed it with *Echoes of the People* both under the Gentlethunder name and self -released.

One of my own personal and proudest moments, and I am sure Simon feels the same, is the creation of *Sand Creek......lest we forget.*

It is a story I have carried with me since I was nineteen years old. As a young adult I saw the film Soldier Blue in the local cinema with David, a friend and work colleague. The title song is sung by Buffy Sainte-Marie and it rips your heart out in the same way of the film. It portrays the brutal massacre and slaughter, and mainly of women and children, of the Cheyenne and Arapaho tribes camped peacefully alongside of Sand Creek. Over seven hundred militia slaughtered the Indians for simply being Indians. For no other reason than they were classed as savages. I came out of the cinema in shock and as I walked down the steps outside, I had a tear in my eye and I glanced across at David and he had the same.

At that time, I just thought it was a film made in Hollywood and didn't connect it to a real event. That came much later in life. We made another trip to the States with our friend Susan and we hired another RV to tour through the reservations. By now I was aware of Sand Creek and we found ourselves heading back south and decided to visit the site of the massacre. At that time there was no official site and it was hard to locate the place where it happened. We came across what we knew as the poles of an historic marker but with the sign broken and battered and laying on the ground. It was as if it was being allowed to fade away in to history and become quietly forgotten about. We turned in between the poles and drove down a long dusty road until we came to the end. There were privately owned fields preventing any further vehicle access, but we could see the outline of the creek ahead by the bushes growing alongside. We were all quite angry. It just seemed that history was being wiped away and out of living memory.

We all ventured out of the RV and walked towards the creek. I sat down alone and pondered on what happened there. I was angry, and I could feel it within me. As I sat there, I began to feel my anger change to sadness and slowly evolve in to a resolve to carry on and fight and the pride of the Native American nations. It was a very emotional moment sitting there feeling connected to an event so long ago. My initial anger about the battle and the historic marker had faded away and had been replaced by a great sense of peace. The creek had recovered and once again become a place of peace and I was feeling it.

Years later, when we were making Echoes of the People, I related the story to Simon. He listened quietly and I'm sure he felt my pain. He simply got up and went to the piano and started playing. What came out is *Sand Creek…. lest we forget.* I am immensely proud of that track.

CHAPTER TEN.

Music has always been important to me and is a big part of my life today. I enjoy listening to albums of all genres and I enjoy playing my guitars in my little studio. Playing an instrument didn't come easy for me but I am proud that I never gave up and I enjoy the peace it brings. If I had a bad day at work, after 20 mins of playing my guitar it was all forgotten about. I get absorbed in the playing and it allows a release of the pent-up energy. Time just disappears.

We did some work on an album called "Best of both Worlds" by an Irish folk singer named Ray Moore. He had been in to the local music store to buy strings whilst he was in Aberdeen working and asked about local studios and they put him on to us. He brought two tracks for us to work on. Both tracks just had acoustic guitar and vocals. He asked us to complete the tracks. One was the old Sandy Denny track, "Who knows where the time goes" and the other was a traditional folk song called "the Jeannie C". It was about a fishing boat capsizing and the loss of the crew. Ray has a very beautiful voice and it was a pleasure to help.

I will never forget once we had finished and we called him in to approve our production. We had recorded my electric guitar and Simons piano to enhance the initial tracks. We sat Ray down about six feet in front of the speakers, turned out the light, and played the tracks. The tears that streamed down his face gave us his approval. You know, it is the very simple things in life that leave the longest and lasting impressions. God Bless Ray.

Through my work as a gas engineer I got to meet all sorts of people as I serviced or repaired their boilers. One of those people turned out to be very special to me as I got to know her. Kate was 76 years old when I was given the job to repair her leaking boiler. The boiler was obsolete and one of the parts needed was no longer available so I used sealant to stop the leak. It only lasted a week or so and I was called back again. If I couldn't repair the boiler it would have to be replaced so I did my best once again. About another week later I was called back to the same leak! I decided to drain the system, remove the part and solder it up! That would cure it and would save the boiler from being replaced. I had remarked to Kate that because it kept leaking it looked like divine intervention that we had to meet and she casually replied, "Yes indeed" and so started a lovely friendship.

Kate taught Yoga classes for most of her life and was still teaching them when I met her! She could still do all the moves and age didn't daunt her and she had a young outlook too. Kate also gave light meditation classes to a local cancer care charity and had tried her best to record them on a simple cassette player so that if she couldn't make the evening class they could play the tapes instead. They were obviously done just sitting in a chair and talking at the cassette recorder so the volume came and went as she moved. She asked if I could help her out to do a better recording.

I spoke to Simon about it and we agreed to get her in to the studio to do better recordings of her own meditations. Then the idea came to work together with Kate and add music to them to make it a journey. Kate was thrilled and so we got her in to record her voice. She has a wonderful speaking voice. It's very clear, has great diction and is very soothing. Once we had the words on tape we split it up and added music in between her phrases. We then extended the middle to be just music so you could drift off and follow Kate's guidance. After about 15 minutes or so Kate's voice would come back in to return you to base! It worked really well and we made two guided meditation albums with Kate, "the Bluebell Wood" and "the Mother Star". Kate is the star on them for she brings a very beautiful and peaceful energy to them.

I have been trying to walk a spiritual path for many years and I saw my music as an accompaniment to what I was trying to achieve. It opened doors with people and I received emails from all over the world commenting on the albums and it led to helping others and being helped myself. Whenever you help someone from the heart it is always a two-way thing. Being thanked for helping someone to fit a piece of their jigsaw in to place is always returned by receiving the same gift back. It isn't always apparent at the time, but it is so. Give and you shall receive I think is the phrase. I can remember some of the kind words said to me by customers I would never meet again and yet their words still resonate with me to this day. When words are spoken with kindness they have so much power to heal.

It's the same as seek and you will find. I was seeking but not finding what I was looking for. I have had lots of hobbies in my life from cycling, pot-holing, cave diving, scuba diving, triathlons, fishing, target shooting, parachuting, photography, motorsport and of course music. The only one that has brought great joy and peace is music. I have enjoyed all the others immensely, but music has been with me since childhood and is a constant. The peace it brings to me is real, but it is not a lasting peace. I have to step back in to the world and become immersed in everything that is involved in being a part of it, except I always felt apart *from it*. I have played football and been a team member but always felt not fully involved. I swam for the school in my early teens and was part of the team but never really felt like a full member.

I always felt different. If you say that to most people, they don't hear the word "different", they hear the word "better". They immediately think you are saying "better than" but I wasn't. It was even going the other way in that I felt lesser than. Being better than anyone couldn't be in my vocabulary the way I was feeling by feeling *apart from*. I had no idea that I was feeling apart from *myself* but that would come later. I was a square peg in a round hole.

Like most people, my journey started by looking outwards for the answers. It's easy to think that we will read the right book, go to *that* workshop, join the right group or meet the right people who will give us that light bulb moment. For most of us that doesn't happen. I used to admire friends that I thought were settled in life and outwardly happy, but I realised, in their quiet moments of sharing, that they too were seeking "something" even if they didn't know or admit what it was. In some ways that is comforting, maybe you aren't so different after all, but in other ways it asks more questions. Why are some of us, and perhaps most of us, going through life knowing that something is missing? It begs the question "what is missing?" That's not an easy question to answer and there is no universal answer because each one of us needs to know what it is in varying levels of curiosity.

For myself, the need to know who I am was becoming stronger and stronger. It wouldn't go away and when I let it go and just got on with a physical life it would come back and remind me. I would work on my old classic car and be happy at the progress or buy a new guitar and be happy with the instrument, but it was always a fleeting happiness. There had to be more. There had to be happiness that didn't go away. I know I am not alone. I see it with friends and relatives and it is just the way most of us go through our lives. We buy a new car and for the first few months we wash it weekly and then it tails off to once a month. It is just a normal occurrence and stepping out of normality is a hard and huge step to take. It can't be done out of curiosity. If we know something is missing, we have to reach that point in our lives when we make a decision to find it. It has to be a conscious decision and not an unconscious one. Curiosity is neither one or the other, but it is a step towards the one that will answer our questions. We will end up in one camp or the other.

In helping my young nephew Jake, who is at the curious stage, I realised something very powerful. Something so important in how most of us go through life. As we walked through the woods he asked me questions that I did my best to answer. I had to be gentle and take it slowly so that it didn't overwhelm him. He eventually said that "he wanted to find himself". How many times have we all heard someone say that?

I was about to give an answer, but I found myself holding back. Isn't it the question we have all heard spoken? Isn't it the very reason people set off on this journey? Isn't that what we are all secretly looking for? Who are we? Who is the real us? Who is the real me? Who am I?

I thought about it for a few moments and found myself giving a different answer than the one I expected to give.

I told him that he had *already* found himself. I said that what he really needed to do was *experience* himself.

In trying to find ourselves it implies that there is another Being separate to ourselves and that the very act of *trying to find* could involve a sense of *failing to find*. It would be a big disappointment on our journey if we never walked in to a room and saw ourselves waiting there, or to look in every doorway for a Being that we see separate to ourselves but never come to meet. *That thought process automatically invites failure*. We already have everything we need right here and right now. In my desire to help Jake I was helping myself. It is always the way. If we give out from the heart, we receive the same back. It made me think very hard on what I had said.

We need to experience what we already have inside of us. There is nothing separate from us, what we are looking for is *already a part of us*. The part of us we seek is already within and we just need to *experience it*. Once we grasp that, and I mean really grasp it, then there is no waiting anymore. There is no looking anymore only experiencing. We can start experiencing ourselves immediately. Right now, in this very moment. We start to become aware of ourselves. We become aware of how we think, how we act and how that effects the image we project in to the world. *We actually start living in awareness from that very moment*. It may sound very simple, very trite but almost all the powerful truths in the world are made simple so that all of us can understand. They are made with the innocence of a child in mind and yet we don't see it.

I started to really believe that I could find my answers. I was already aware and awake to a bigger picture, but I wasn't consciously and actively a part of it. I felt *apart* from it. I started to ask myself why. I realised my biggest hurdle to overcome was my past. I wanted to find my inner Truth. I didn't want a glimpse of it, I wanted *all* of it. I wanted to connect fully with my spirit because I knew my spirit was connected to the Source or God or the Collective Consciousness or whatever word you choose to describe the bigger picture. I believe in a Creator, that this world isn't a happy accident, and so I use the word God to describe a Greater Being than myself and yet who I am part of because of my spirit which is the gift of life. I needed to *feel* it. I knew it, but I had to *experience it*. It had to be all or nothing for me. If we dwell on the past it makes that need to have it all seem like an impossible task. I knew I wasn't perfect. I alone knew of all of my failings and I was, and am, far from perfect.

I then realised if I waited for perfect it would never happen. *You can't wait for Perfect.*

I couldn't go back and erase all my wrong doings. It is impossible. I had to deal with them once and for all. I started by examining how I behaved now and how I thought about things now. Everything we do starts with a thought. If we want a cup of tea, we think about it first and then we take action and make the cup of tea. We then experience the result. Now, I already knew this. *We* already know it. We all know that is how life works. We think about it, we do it and it happens. We don't think about breathing because it happens unconsciously but if we want to *Be* in our lives we *must think consciously*. We all know this. Most of us don't follow it. I did it when it suited me.

It was time to really start to live consciously. It meant pausing before I replied to a question. The pause gave me the choice to think about what I was going to say and sometimes my first thought just faded away as the *right* thought came. It was uncomfortable. I found myself being shocked at some of my initial thoughts and it began to feel like there were two of us. I realised it was bad wolf and good wolf both trying to be heard only this time I *really* realised what was going on inside of me. I tried to feed the good wolf and I could if I wasn't under stress and had time to think. Under pressure or in a difficult situation it was much harder. I started to realise that I was slowly changing. I started to allow myself that acknowledgement. It wasn't easy. In trying to have better thoughts I started to react differently to set situations that almost always previously brought negativity. I won, and I lost. At least winning *sometimes* was a start.

I became involved with a close family member who had taken on a project and needed help in getting it off the ground. It is far too personal for either of us to go in to details, but it didn't work out. It didn't work out for either party and I had to walk away. It was a very negative situation for both of us and because it was the very last thing I wanted at that stage of my life, I withdrew. That is not to say that it was because of the other party, it was not. Neither of us knew why it was happening, but it was, and was hurting us both. Walking away was the best thing to do for all of us.

I have no resentment or negative attachment to it anymore for it eventually brought me the freedom and truth I had been seeking. It brought me to my knees in every sense.

When I withdrew it left me with time on my hands and it also gave me time to heal. As a teenager I never had a conversation with my Father. Children were to be seen and not heard and the only thing I heard was being told what to do. If he was going to watch a rugby match, and I asked to go, he would just say No, he was going with his friends and having a pint afterwards and he couldn't take me. It was just the way it was and all I knew. As a teenager I had no idea what my own Fathers upbringing had been like. It was never talked about. He was orphaned at 14 years old having lost his Father and his Mother a few years earlier. In those days there wasn't the same social services and he just went to live with his older sister Mary. When he was fifteen years of age he got a job on the railway and soon after moved in to lodgings when he became sixteen. That must have been truly difficult at his age and I didn't appreciate it for I only found out a lot of things about my Father later in life. Later I became very close to my Father as far as my feelings towards him. At some point I must have realised that being a Father is not easy and I know under his own circumstances he did the best he could. He never told me he loved me whilst he was alive. Not once. Even when I was dying in the ambulance, he couldn't say it. When he came back in spirit it was the very first thing he said to me "I love you" but I always knew he did. I love you so much Dad.

As a Father I tried to do better with my own two children. I took them fishing, cycling and air-rifle target shooting and on many other adventures too. Lynn has said that perhaps I only took them because I was going too but that's not the truth. Only I know that. It would have been much easier to have gone on my own so that when away for the long weekends at a shooting match I wouldn't have to pay for three shares of the petrol, three lots of meals, three entries and three competition air-rifles etc. I could have just gone with my mates with no parental responsibility. My kids came with me and I enjoyed that they enjoyed it too. It had a price though. A Father behaves differently when he is out with his friends than he does with his children. They saw me outside of being a Father and then the Father returned when we got home. It wasn't easy for either party.

I entered the project with every intention of making up for any failings I have had with my children. My own father was very heavily on my mind and I wanted to do better. As I said previously, for whatever reasons the good intent never came to anything and the pain of my own childhood and history almost repeating itself became too much. I had to take a long hard look at my life and I had to heal myself. I cracked. I just felt so much despair and the feeling of being so alone. It was as if everything I had earned, bought and worked for in life just meant nothing. It seemed like a wasted life and there had to be more. It really made me question why I felt like that. This wasn't me feeling sorry for myself. I had a good life, a house that we own and all the physical trappings that working brings. This was an emptiness *inside*. It seemed that all my attempts to walk a spiritual path had come to nothing. There was a void inside of me and the gap to reaching *me* seemed to be as wide as it was when I started.

I love walking Becky in our woods behind the house. Well they feel like *our* woods anyway! I take it in turn with Lynn and I always enjoy my turn. I go the same route every day, Lynn calls it the Roman road, but I know if I stray, I would get lost. I can't find my car in a car park. I feel part of the woods, I see trees as being very much alive and walking amongst the trees began to heal my soul. I have a special tree, it's very old, battered and scarred but it is so beautiful because of it. It has seen *life* in the woods and I always spend time with it as I pass. Just holding one of the broken branches and simply going quiet and in to the stillness releases any negativity and I always walk away with a sense of peace. I began to heal. Slowly I began putting everything I had learned about spirituality in to practice. It was very slow at first, and by not beating myself up when I "failed", I could feel progress within me.

We all see "inspirational" messages on social media and we can all identify with some that touched us or provoked us in to thinking about it a little longer than it took the time to read it. It is feeling that gentle prod and acting on it. The one that really hit me was the one I have spoken about before, the Good wolf and the Bad wolf. It really hit home because it is so simple to understand, and I could see it happening within myself. It was time to act on it. This time I was really starting to think about how I think, how I act and how I feel.

I started to dwell on Black Elks teachings.

I had read his book several times and the knowledge contained within was starting to come out. He said that "**in the centre of the Universe dwells the Great Spirit"** and he also said, "**and the centre of the Universe is wherever we are standing"**.

It means that where ever we are, we are at One with the Universe and we don't need to be in a specific location. The location of our truth and our answer's dwells within Us. We own and take them everywhere we go. Black Elk's way of seeing the Great Spirit all around him in nature and people made his relationship with the Great Spirit very real and very personal and a way of life. Although he became a Catechist later in life and worked on behalf of the Catholic church, it was his closeness to the Great Spirit that made his teachings in and out of church very real to him. He recognised that his Great Spirit and God were the same and the creator of all things. He was teaching to fellow Native Americans on the reservation and his understanding of both sides of the coin would surely have helped those around him to understand. At that time Christianity was being forced on to them and he must have helped so many to come to terms with it and find a way through it without losing who they were.

He also says, **"and in the centre of the Universe there grows a Sacred tree"** and I began to experience it as I walked through the woods. I began to experience the Sacred Tree within my inner being as the Soul within me, and I began to feel the seeds of the fruit growing within me. He had said that "when we water the tree it will bear fruit" and I was watering my tree. I started to really look forward to the walks with Becky as it took me to my sacred space and I also started going out on my own at times. I started to see the trees in a different light, literally, and I could see them as living *beings* and part of the very earth I was standing on. They really *were* part of it all and I began to become grounded and feel that I was part of it all too. It was so strong that I found myself just grinning at the wonder of it all. Walking with a crazy smile on my face as I looked at a simple flower or a shrub and marvelled at the little birds that flew around me and having to stifle the smile as a walker came towards me.

I started to take that feeling of peace and belonging away from me when I left the woods. It only stayed briefly as life always got in the way, but it was taking a deeper hold on me and the peace was growing within.

Years previously I had written a song that we recorded about Black Elks teachings. It was called the "Beauty of the Forest" and how apt, that almost twenty years later, all the words of the song were coming true. It's about Oneness and Wholeness. It's about revealing the true Self.

The beauty of the forest is *within* the Sacred tree. One tree does not make a forest and yet the forest cannot be a forest without the single tree. We all make up the forest and each one of us is part of the Whole and yet each one of us contains the beauty of it All. One cannot exist without the other.

The first two lines of the song had always haunted me and there were many times I had reflected on it. It always made me wonder where the words came from as I wrote them down. It's also most likely the first thing I play when I pick up a guitar.

"*There will come a time, when I will hold my key, and all the faces I have shown you, well none of them were me.*

"*and all the pain I hold in my heart will one day set me free…to feel the beauty all around, that I never thought I would see*"

I needed to find my key. The key I needed to unlock the secrets of my soul and the answers I needed. I had to find that key.

CHAPTER ELEVEN.

I continued to walk the woods with Becky and the feelings of being connected grew stronger and stronger. I felt a part of the woods, as if it was my safe and sacred space. I wasn't just walking through the woods passively anymore but actively engaging in it. I came to know almost every tree as I passed them and would just smile as I walked by. Once, I came across a tree that had been blown over in the night by the strong winds and the tip of the tree, that previously reached far in to the sky above, just touched the edge of the path at my feet. I reached down to touch it and I felt so sad at it lying there. I was holding the newest growth of the tree that had taken all summer to grow and it seemed such a waste. I looked around and there was no one close by, and so I said out loud *"Please help me to raise the tree again, nobody will know, there's just us"* but nothing happened. I looked at the tree and was feeling the loss and as I started to walk away, I thought *"I'm sorry I can't fix you"* and then a very serine and gentle voice said, *"But it is not broken".* It stopped me in my tracks and I repeated the words to myself over and over. After the initial shock I pondered at the *significance* of what was said. The tree was a part of it all, it was just being a tree, it had grown and experienced a life in the woods and was now lying down to return to the earth and become the very soil for the next tree that would grow from the tiny pine cones around it.

It was telling me that *everything was just as it should be.* Life is a cycle and life and death are a natural part of that process. I would walk past the tree daily afterwards, and eventually the green branches faded to brown as the tree willingly let go. I didn't feel sad anymore. It was a simple lesson about life and death given to me by nature, the nature I was starting to feel a part of and not apart from anymore. I began to understand more about myself and I began the first steps of truly walking in harmony with myself. It always starts with ones self first.

The woods are my meditation. Annette has always said I was a walking meditation and I was starting to agree with her! I just go quiet there and I can reach in to the stillness fairly quickly. Until that is, I get a nudge at my pocket from Becky because it's biscuit time. She knows to stop at certain trees and wait until I get there for a pitstop. Some pitstops are two biscuits long. I can forget my woes and just enjoy the peace of the moment. I was thinking about the key, the one I would hold from the song, that would unlock the door to everything. I knew it wasn't a physical key but a metaphoric one but what did I have to do to find it? What process did I have to put in place to find the greatest treasure I was seeking? I didn't know the answer. I kept pondering on it and in that very act I knew I was seriously beginning to seek my answers. I was beginning to think better, act better and to *feel* better.

I was walking one day, as usual with Becky, and I just stopped suddenly. The penny dropped. Out of nowhere came the thought that *I was the key! I already had the key to everything I needed to know and experience!* I already knew this as a concept but I didn't really accept it and believe it yet Jesus had said "*and the Kingdom of Heaven is within you*" and in a different language and words, Black Elk had said *"in the centre of the Universe dwells the Great Spirit and the centre of the Universe is wherever you are standing"* and right in that moment I stood there in the centre of my universe and I felt the Kingdom of Heaven within me. Right then and right there, I knew that *I was the key* and that all I had to do was to put it in my lock and open the door to the kingdom within. I just had to *choose* to do it. It wasn't just a case of thinking it, it was a case of feeling it and knowing it and believing in that I really did hold the key to open my own inner door. The feeling coursed through my entire body and I knew that I was accepting the concept at last.

In that moment I finally came to the absolute realisation that we do have all the answers within us. It is the birth right for *every one of Us, not just for some of Us, but for all of Us*. As I walked, I felt the key being turned in my inner door and I felt it sink in to my whole being and thought process. There was a change within and I could feel it. As I walked further, I realised that every door within that I needed to open no longer needed a key. *I just had to open it.*

It is one thing to know intellectually that we hold our own answers, but it doesn't feel real until we feel it. Once we feel it, we experience it and draw that experience towards us and then there is no going back. At least there wasn't for me. It was becoming real.

I don't know the exact moment it happened, but I was walking along the path with Becky in front of me, and I started to feel energy around me and it grew in strength until all I could see was a beautiful and iridescent light surrounding me and it seemed to be emitting from me. It was so strong that I could hardly see through it as it grew stronger and stronger. The feelings inside of me were indescribable. I felt that I was taking each step in Grace, in the presence of something greater than me, and it was blissful. It was sheer and utter bliss. I felt ecstatic and at total peace and *nothing else mattered*. There wasn't a past or a future, there was only that blissful moment and a feeling of being very much a part of *everything.* There was no separation, no feeling *apart from*, just the absolute joy of *being a part of everything*.

It lasted for a few days. It poured through every part of my body and nothing got in its way. I was experiencing the most wonderous joy, peace and love that couldn't even be imagined in my wildest moments.

I will try to describe what bliss felt like to me. Words won't be able to express how I felt and how I felt connected to everything. I will try but I know I can't write it down adequately. As hard as I try to convey it I will fail.

You know when you have the great desire to reach your greatest goal, to act out your most treasured dream? When everything you have strived for comes within reach and you *know* you are going to experience your most cherished desire that you have nurtured for most of your life?

Well bliss is nothing like that.

Bliss is in the simplest of things.

Bliss was in tying my boot laces and being totally in that moment, *there was nothing else*. Becky was wagging her tail because she knew the boots meant "walkies", but I was living in the joy of watching my fingers tie the knots. *There was nothing else.* That was my *life* in that moment and I was *living* it. Living in the moment of closing the gate quietly behind me so as not to wake the neighbours and feeling the joy of the clasp closing quietly with a click. Smiling to myself whilst watching Becky twenty yards in front of me and almost in the woods. I was enjoying walking those twenty yards in total joy for I was *living* those twenty yards. There really was nothing else but that moment. It felt precious, it felt beautiful and I felt alive and connected to everything. The trees connected to my own energies and I felt at One with the world.

Life wouldn't start when I reached the woods, *life was happening to me on the journey to the woods.*

Every step I took was in the *now and within my own life* as it happened within real time. I wasn't apart from my life anymore I *was* my life! There was nothing in my thoughts except the wonderment of taking the next step forward and being *in* my life and being *life itself.* I was smiling within, but I was grinning ecstatically outwardly too. I was experiencing life as it should be and living my life in full consciousness and experiencing it in all its simple splendour and joy. I was *being* the Being that I am. Bliss is a word that sums up those feelings.

I said I couldn't convey in words what I felt, and reading it back only scratches the surface of what It felt like. Words are inadequate at conveying feelings for we experience through our feelings and not through our words.

Bliss lasted for a few days and then I felt it slowly fade away but not everything went with it. I was left with a sense of peace, a deeper peace than I had ever felt before, and I knew it was, at some point, to become permanent and not fleeting. *I was on to something here and I wasn't about to let it go.*

Years ago, whenever I had experienced something spiritual, I felt like I was holding on to a fine gossamer thread that I wanted to pull on gently to get closer to the truth, but it felt like that thread could break at any moment. That thread later turned in to rope and now it was a chain and no amount of tugging could break it. I was going to pull on this chain for all I was worth.

I've read many inspirational books and some of them I have read twice. I always learn something, and I know that in the reading of some of them, seeds were being planted.

A truly inspiring book is "The Power of Now" by Eckhart Tolle. It triggered something inside of me, but I wasn't ready then to put it in to practice.

 Another series of books that had a huge impact on me was the "Conversations with God" books by Neal Donald Walsch. These really hit home because they presented a God that felt real to me and attainable. A God that would approach me on terms that I could understand and, more importantly, would accept me for who I am. It didn't matter to me if it *was* God who dictated those books because the truth they contain is simply the Truth and that is what mattered to me.

Many years ago I watched a television programme about two lesbians. It was two people very much in love and dedicated to each other. It was late at night and as I turned the TV off and wondered off up to bed, I was thinking about it. I lay awake thinking. I finally just asked "Father, what do you *really* think about that?" That very quiet, calm and serene voice replied, *"It is better to project Love in to the world than bigotry and hatred"*

Wow! What a profound statement. It was spinning around in my head, but I realised it was a truth that couldn't be argued with. Not by anyone. Not by any head of Church or State, any doctrine or person. It really *was* better to project Love than any bigotry or hatred. It applies to everything we do, and in every situation and it was given in such a simple way. It is the lowest common denominator and can't be argued with because if we do, we are saying the very opposite to Love.

It especially applies to any situation where racism and prejudice of any kind are involved. It doesn't matter what colour or creed, whether rich or poor or whatever religious persuasion is involved, the answer to the problem is always the same: *It is better to project Love in to the world than bigotry and hatred*. If we allow bigotry and hatred to overrule Love, then we as a human race and the planet that supports us are doomed to fail. Bigotry and hatred divide us, but Love unites us. How do we as one person remove hatred and bigotry from our world? We do it by removing them from ourselves. How do we climb a mountain? *By taking one step at a time.*

Was it the voice of God I heard? I have no idea. It didn't and doesn't matter to me because I was *hearing the Truth*. I was also *feeling* the Truth contained within it and that is what matters.

I am a very practical person. I served time as an apprentice to become a Gasfitter and I later turned that in to becoming a mechanic and then back to a Gasfitter. They are both practical and down to earth jobs.

I would lie under a very shallow floor trying to change a central heating pump, with water dripping up my sleeve and on to my face, and then come back out covered in glass wool insulation and itching like crazy. It doesn't get more practical than that and so the kind of person that I am needs to understand how things work. I couldn't understand anything about spirituality if it was given to me in an esoteric and fairy-tale way. It had to have substance that I *could understand*. Understanding the deeper mysteries of the universe can only come once the basics are understood and assimilated in to our lives. We might learn how to add and subtract but that doesn't mean we can understand advanced calculus. We need solid building blocks of understanding otherwise our sand castle may return to sand.

I realised that I wasn't alone in this. Most very ordinary and very normal people need to be given it in a way that can be seen to be useable and I am one of those people. Whilst such things as meditation can bring great peace and understanding, telling that to the average carpenter, plumber or checkout girl might not have any impact or meaning in their lives when given as practical advice. The spiritual building blocks need to be put in to place so that meditation can then be seen as a part of good spiritual practice.

I needed to break it all down. I needed to condense everything that had touched me, from reading a book, meeting a person, experiencing the divine and the seeking of myself. I needed to gather everything learned in to a form that could be passed on and in a way that would be practical and workable without altering any fundamental truths. It shouldn't be such a big task......but joking aside, I needed to do it. If I could work it out for myself it could also apply to anyone who chooses to use it as a guideline.

There is nothing I am going to tell you that is new. There is nothing that some of you haven't read already or heard spoken of. All I want to do is to encourage you to take those first curious steps and, in a way that you can slowly see progress.

I am sorry for turning *We* in to *You* and writing to *You*. It is not because I am writing from the lofty heights of already being here, it is because I want to speak to *you* personally. *You* are Me. There is no difference. My journey is your journey and your journey is my journey too. We are united in our search for the truth. We are all on the meaningful journey of life.

So, *what is the meaning of life?*

The meaning of life is to *live* your life. To *live it* in a fully conscious way and then you *become* your life. You are no longer *separated from it* for you are *all of it.* To live your life in the present and in the presence of the Being you really are. There is no separation anymore from *anything* because you are *everything.*

What is my life's purpose? When will I find my true purpose in life?

You will find your true purpose in life when you *live* your life. A life lived in full awareness of *life itself* can only lead to a life *purposefully lived.* Your life purpose will become abundantly clear to you simply by the way you act and the path you choose to walk. You are now living a life *with a purpose* and a meaning to it and all will unfold before you. Doors will open naturally, and you will choose which doors you wish to pass through.

CHAPTER TWELVE.

This is now becoming *our* journey and we are sharing the rest of this book together.

 I am not "in front" of you. I am alongside of you. I am merely one breath ahead of you until you decide to breathe in and join me. The one breath it takes to write it down. That is all. Just one breath, and you can take that breath any time you choose. *I have been at that point many times in my life but have not had the courage to take it.* I have read many self-help books, just like this one, and although they all touched me, it was mostly on an unconscious level and I never had the courage to breathe in to it. *I finally took that breath and breathed in to a new life.*

It really is that simple. I chose to change. I chose to fill the void within me. I had to find the part of me that was missing, and I realised it was the connection between *me* and my *real* Self. I had been walking the physical path of life in parallel with a spiritual path. At times I had to devote time to the physical aspects of life and then be free to indulge in spiritual life but that created the void in between! **The part of me that was missing was the connection between the two paths**. I had to make it the one path, *the only path.* I knew in my heart that there was a greater being within me for my soul was crying out to me and I was hearing it through the pain within. I had to connect to that Greater Being if I wanted to find peace. I had now finally understood and accepted the part of me that was missing and I began to combine both paths in to one. I would try to live life as One being. A being at One with itself.

I have written about my life up to this point and I have tried to show you what kind of person is writing this book. I have shared some of the highs and lows of my life and yet some things must remain private. The writing of this book has healed many scars from my past. As I have written it down, I have experienced the pain all over again. It has, at times, brought me to tears and it has nearly stopped me from writing. There have been occasions when I had to almost force myself to write because I knew if I didn't the Bad wolf would have won again. I am human, I have failings, but I *am allowed to change*. I just needed to allow myself.

I am now entering in to unknown territory because so far, I have written what I know about and that is my life. I am qualified to write about that. My life is changing for the better and it is happening quickly, very quickly, and so much so, that even I must accept it, and I give thanks for the help I am receiving both outwardly and from within.

What is changing about my life? I am finding peace and it is becoming a lasting peace. It is no longer fleeting. I am learning to let go of anger, resentment, envy, and most importantly fear. It is an ongoing journey, but I am at last *enjoying* the journey. I try to live my life in the moment and not *when I get "there"*.

Where is "there"? Where is this place called "there" that is so magical that we will live our lives once we get "there"? We set off to the cinema and we will enjoy the movie once we get "there". The journey to the cinema is just as important. If it isn't as important, then the life that we live whilst driving "there", isn't important also. It just happens. Life just **happens** on the way to the cinema, but it **starts** once we get there! That is living life on auto pilot or in an unconscious awareness of life. **There is life on the way**. It changes *everything* once we realise that every single, unconscious breath we take, is giving us the chance of a *conscious* life. If we choose to accept this, we live a life we have chosen and not one *that just happens*. We *become our life* and are not separate to it. We take control and we *choose* our outcome instead of the one that just *happens to us.*

I have asked that this book be written in such a way that it encourages people to see that anyone can unlock the key to themselves by carrying out some simple self-analysis. I am not a psychiatrist and will not be delving in to the depths of the unconscious mind. I want to use words and examples that everyone can understand even if it looks like I am simplifying the greater mysteries too much. I just want to pass on, and in ways that will help to start to live a life in full consciousness, of who *we really* are. Who *we really are* will become *ours to decide.*

We need to start by pondering on how we Think.

 If we sit comfortable and relaxed and say to ourselves "I am going to sit for one minute without thinking about *anything*" we will find it almost impossible to do. Thoughts will pop in to our heads like traffic in the rush hour. We will find ourselves experiencing the most unlikely and strangest of thoughts and will silently ask "where did that come from". The truth is, that by trying to do that simple act for just one minute, we will *experience* how we think. In just one minute, we will realise that we can't control our thoughts. That's all it will take out of your life to *experience* this. Everyone has one minute to spare. Not only can we not *control* them we can't even *stop* them! Thoughts are very powerful, and they always precede any action we make. Even if the action is for us to do nothing at all we have to think it first. Thoughts create scenarios and sometimes that can be dangerous because the ego needs to act out the scenario that our thoughts created.

Thoughts always precede any Action.

I have said earlier that even the simple act of making coffee begins with the thought "I need a coffee". If we are watching television and we get up to make coffee automatically, we are doing it from an unconscious thought. We need to think consciously and act out the thought in a conscious manner and not be on auto pilot which is how *most of us live our lives*. If we want a positive outcome from our thoughts, we must have positive thoughts. If we *consciously choose* to make coffee, we are living our life as we make it. That small amount of time it takes to make coffee is just as important as the time we have when we drink it. If it isn't important, we have *chosen* to not *consciously* experience that part of our lives. We are on auto pilot and not living in full awareness of life. Awareness starts with the easy and small things in life. This allows it to be noticed, it allows us to notice that we are aware of making coffee and we become aware of the greater things in life too.

Thoughts and actions lead us to our experiences.

We **think** we would like to see a movie. We **act** by driving to the cinema and then we **experience** the movie. *It is such a simple process and that is how life works*. It doesn't matter that the thought is a more complex thought, it still leads to an action and that may lead to a more complicated experience, but that is how we and life work.

Is it not better, therefore, to choose better thoughts to achieve a more thoughtful action to bring a more pleasant experience? It makes sense.

When we decide to start living a conscious life that we *choose,* it is not easy at first, but it does slowly become easier. Sitting quietly and trying to still our thoughts seems like an impossible task. It is very easy to be discouraged. We find we are bombarded with thoughts and it seems that immediately we try to slow them down the more they come! *That is normal.* That is the ego realising you are on a path to letting go of it and it *does not like it.* We think we are what we *think* we are, and have no choice in the outcome, but we are *no*t who we think we are. **Our thoughts are influenced by both sides of us**. Once again, I am making it simple, but we have the Good wolf and the Bad wolf at play. Except that it isn't a game, it is a battle, and both have a deep desire to win. **The one you feed will win.**

Most of us feel that battle within. It is a very real battle, and there must be, *and will be*, an outcome. We are given the freewill to *choose* that outcome. *There is a life ahead no matter which side we choose.* **Life will not stop**. If we *choose* to leave the battle to continue, we will feel the battle raging inside of us, and we will continue with our lives as we have always done. Life will not stop but it can't bring peace except in fleeting moments. If we want to find eternal peace and experience it, we must choose to feed the Good wolf only. It is that simple.

It is the battle of our ego and our Higher Self. We must start slowly at first, or we will become discouraged. Each thought we choose for the better is a step on the pathway to peace. How do we climb a mountain? Yes…. I know you know the answer.

Everyone reading this can take that first step.

We can never remove the ego from our Being, but we can choose to not be influenced by it unless we *choose* it. It is like the battery leads of our cars and if we remove either the positive or the negative connection the car will not work. We need both to complete the circuit. Within ourselves we need the ego and the Higher Self to make us *complete,* otherwise, **we have no free will.** We need to have the freedom of being able to make a choice. We are given the freedom to express our freewill in any way we choose. *We all have that freedom.* It is in the way we express it that decides *who we are in any given moment.*

There came a point in my battle when I knew which side was winning. It spurred me on to try harder and to become a better person for I was seeing and feeling the results of my efforts. I was experiencing it as I functioned in life. It was genuine progress and it was bringing peace and humility. A humility in accepting that even a person like me, who has made many mistakes, deserved peace.

I was in the woods one day and as usual I was meditating whilst I walked, and I "saw" the outcome of my battle. I was walking at peace with myself, deep in thought and feeling part of the forest and I saw the Bad wolf lying on the ground in submission, its force spent, and I raised my sword to deliver the final and fatal blow. As my sword reached high above me and was ready to make that final downward swing, I stopped. **I could not slay my wolf. Instead I threw down the sword and embraced the wolf and loved him with all of my heart for I was loving *a part of me.*** It would have been like slaying my inner child and I could not do such a thing. **In that moment I experienced an even deeper sense of peace**. It took a few days for it to sink in that I had finally made peace with myself and was in *acceptance of all that I Am.* I was finally *accepting* all of my past failures and realising that all of them had brought me to where I was standing now. The peace has remained.

The Bad wolf remains inside of me, and always will, for he is a part of me. I feed him enough for him to feel loved and keep him safe and warm just as if he were a child. I do not wish to harm him, and he is content with remaining in the background. He barks occasionally, and I just smile and acknowledge his presence and tell him that I love him. I would be heartbroken if he was not there to remind me of who I once was. I just choose not to let those thoughts influence me.

CHAPTER THIRTEEN.

All our thoughts, actions and experiences are interwoven and are all taking place at the same time. There is no separation because we jump from one to the other all the time. There is also a fourth consideration and that is the act of Being. Once we start this journey this is the most complex one for we can choose to be at any time. **Sometimes we must just Be**.

If we take up an apprenticeship to be a carpenter, at the end of it we will have gained the skills and knowledge to become a carpenter and we will have certificates to show that we have the right to work as a carpenter. **Life has no such qualifications**. If we want to become our self, we must *be* our self. If we want to be a good person, we must become a good person. If we want to change our lives, we must be prepared to accept who or what we are changing in to and we must be that person. That is easier said than done because we are all so very hard on ourselves. If we see a friend struggling, we reach out instantly to help them, but we find it hard to see that we ourselves are deserving of such help. Most people find it hard to look in to the mirror and just say "I love you" to the person being reflected back at them. It is easy to say it in a light-hearted way but to look in to our own eyes and see the being that is reflected at us, and to accept all that we see, can be hard for some of us. It is also hard for our friends and relatives because as soon as we declare we want to change we can be seen as a threat in some way. That itself is a crazy notion, but they may find it hard to accept the change because we have stepped out of the box they are carrying with everything they know about us. It can be unnerving for them, but we still must pursue our journey. It is after all our journey. The only permission we need is our own. If we are choosing to put our own box down we must allow others to put theirs down too. It is not about forgiving them for holding our box for that is attaching some blame to them, it is about forgiving ourselves and then there is no need to forgive anyone else for there is nothing to forgive.

This book is intended to be written in the form of a step by step guide to become who we really are. This isn't easy to do because it makes it all sound so clinical, but I want these chapters written in such a way that they can be gone back to and seen as an encouraging reference point as many times as needed. These steps are interchangeable, and it can all occur at once, just as enlightenment can come in the next breath we take. **Who we really are is not a decision made *outside* of ourselves, it is a decision made *within* ourselves**. *We* **choose who we want to Be**. The Universe, the collective consciousness or, in my case God, is not deciding how far we go on this inner journey, it is us that decides. ***Don't brush that off lightly***. If we keep up the practice of experiencing ourselves daily there will come a time when we can't deny that a change within us is taking place and it brings a sense of inner calm. Once peace comes to our lives we are free to live our lives without outer distraction and without being distracted we see the bigger picture. We could say we are a Being without distraction.

My personal journey is to take me to connect with my soul, to experience that part of me that is Holy and only wants the very best for me. I want to reach that place inside of me where my Creator awaits in the form of my Higher Self. *That part of me that was given to me at birth, and when I lay this body down, I know will remain and journey onwards*. I have already experienced my Spirit when I observed myself after the car crash. That experience came out of adversity but now my journey needs to connect consciously with my Spirit because that is *who I really am*. I make no apologies for making it clear I want to go home whilst still in this life. I am also aware that not everybody believes in God or a Greater Being than themselves and I accept and honour this. The choice of believing or not has to be up to each individual and I have no desire to convert anyone. I am simply telling my story and what I believe.

I do not want to preach to anyone, I just want to tell how it is for me. I have also realised that this book can still help those who don't believe. Whilst it is my truth I am telling, I don't want to leave anyone out who may be helped by taking control of their lives without having to believe. Anyone who has sought counselling knows that a good Councillor unravels the problem and takes us to a place of dealing with it without ever mentioning God. By being able to talk openly with a person we trust releases the toxic energy surrounding that problem, and by working on it together, in most cases we can be brought to a place where we can deal with it. This almost always brings peace to the situation and that is where all this is leading. Peace is peace, and it doesn't matter what brings it, because the feeling of safety within us is something we all need. When I finally made a conscious effort to change myself, I gave it commitment. We say we are going on a diet tomorrow knowing that we aren't, but it brings us hope that miraculously the fat will fall away on its own. It doesn't. When I did finally make my decision, and for the tenth time, I knew this time that I meant it. That is all it took, a serious commitment. I started to find that inner peace just through change. That peace was, and is, real. **I stepped in to my**

life instead of walking parallel to it. This alone is worthy of working towards because you do begin to live life whilst awake and not asleep. Slowly we become in charge of our lives and not a consequence of it. That itself is worth the journey for it changes us for the better. *I needed that change.* I also need to go further and deeper. **I know not everybody will feel that need and that is fine because we each choose how far we want to take it. There is no hierarchy in this. We are all the same. We came in to this world in the same way and we go out of it in the same way. What happens in between is up to us.**

 I have clearly nailed my colours to the mast and yet I have realised that this book is for anyone and everyone no matter what their belief system is. Finding inner peace is simply winning the battle of the ego. It simply brings balance in to our lives. The battle with the ego is a psychological battle with the self and does not need to involve an inner or outer presence. Becoming at One with the Universe, however, does require opening the inner door to reach the Soul. It is our choice how far we wish to go on this journey.

I am not going to deny God to make others feel comfortable about the word. I am also not going to force God on to anyone. Take from the book what you choose to take or ignore it completely. All is good and peace to everyone.

I found it easier to start with how I thought. In fact, it is the very best place to start and is non-invasive. We can do it anywhere. How I thought is how I thought of myself as a person. Whilst sitting quietly and alone I would become painfully aware of how much I thought and what I thought about, and how it interacted with my actions and how I thought that was how I determined my life. That must just be *me* having those thoughts and what could I do about it? I would practice becoming "thoughtless", but I could only go for a few seconds mostly. I just had too many thoughts! Slowly the time "between" thoughts would grow a little and then a thought would pop in, usually something crazy like remembering a T-shirt I bought 25 years ago on holiday, but then I began to realise that I was *aware* of that thought coming in. That few seconds of being in the quiet zone created a space that allowed me to be aware of the thought that just entered, and I realised I was beginning to *observe* how I thought. *This made a difference*. I kept on practicing and once I managed to relax and find a few seconds of quiet I would be aware of the next thought and I would observe it. I couldn't analyse it for I did not know why my mind wanted to remind me of the time I grazed my knee in the school playground. I just observed how I thought. It became so that it felt like "another" me was doing the observing. It seemed quite natural when this happened for I was just the *quiet observer*. I felt very peaceful and detached from it and in fact that was what I was doing, I was detaching myself from my thoughts. **So, if they were my thoughts, who was doing the observing?** I had experienced this before in brief moments and I had read enough books to know we have a Higher Self and I connected the two together, but this seemed to be the first time that I was consciously experiencing the real me, even if it was very faintly. I have had experiences of this throughout my life, but I didn't seem to be in control of when they happened. They just happened. **This time I was consciously beckoning myself forward**. It was very faint and very tentative at first, but it grew stronger the more I tried it. My inner being was still distant, but I knew it was there. Becoming *aware of my awareness* acknowledged it and it became a way of connecting to my inner being that I could practice whenever I chose to do so. At first the conversation is one way and I didn't seem to receive any answers, or at least not in a form I recognised. Very slowly I began to realise that my thoughts were slowing down in their intensity and the space between them grew. This made me more aware of the "next" thought that came in. I couldn't stop them from entering my mind, but I realised I could *choose how I dealt with them*. If it was reminding me of being late for an appointment I naturally acted upon it but if it was just meaningless verbiage I just let it go right out of my mind without retaining it. **I gave it no thought or substance and so it had no effect on me. It was gone and out of my mind.**

This practice of slowing down my thoughts became very real to me and I saw progress. It is in fact the basis of all meditation in that we empty our minds and sit in the stillness of our being. I could never become so quiet whenever I tried to meditate. This was my way of connecting to myself, but it became more tangible the more I practiced. I could also practice it wherever I was and whatever situation I was in. **This meant I didn't have to set prescribed times aside and that made sense to me because *life is happening all the time* and not just when we want to be in it**. The space between thoughts also created a pause. It gave me time to think of a response in a conscious manner. That is, when I remembered to do it! It just takes time and practice. Nothing more than that.

Now, if I could become the conscious observer of my thoughts then I could choose which thoughts to act up on. It is amazing what goes through our minds when we start to observe it. From our thoughts we create scenarios and our ego wants to act those scenarios out like a play we have written. ***This can be a good and a bad thing***.

Scenarios can be positive or negative in their forming. If we think about a friend that needs our help we can formulate a plan in our mind to help them. It might mean finding a few hours to visit and just being a listener or it could be of more practical help. Either way the scenario we are creating is a positive one, we want to make it happen, so we act upon it and follow it through. The outcome can't be known but the journey to our friend is filled with good intent. What is just as important is that the time in between having the thought and carrying out our good intent is spent with harmonious thoughts. They do not cause unease within us. We are using our Higher Self in a very natural and caring way, almost as if we don't even need to think about it. It is walking our journey in harmony with ourselves.

The negative scenarios are the ones *to let go of and to stop before they can formulate*. Once they are written in our minds it is very hard not to follow them through just as surely as if they were meant to be. We have written the scene in our mind and we need to act it out. It is our play and we are the leading role. We have had an argument with someone and we reflect on it afterwards. We realise if only we had said this and that we would have won, and if only we could repeat the argument, but this time armed with the right responses, we would come out the winner. **It festers in the mind**. We know we will be seeing this person again soon, and armed with our new and better responses, we want to bring it up again. We meet this person bristling with the need to be proven right and so, as surely as night turns in to day, we find a way of opening the conflict again. Not only have we created a negative scenario where no good can come of it, we have carried it with us and allowed it to fester and grow within our own mind. **We have**

been poisoning our own mind! We have *chosen* to create a negative future when we see this person. ***We must have chosen it, nobody else has, we did***. No matter how heated the argument was previously, it is over, it is in the past so why do we need to re-create it but this time win? It is because our lower self, the ego, is having its say. **The Bad wolf is howling, and we have been listening.** *There is not one person reading this, including and especially myself*, that has not done this repeatedly. Time after time. And then again! ***Just stop it***. Recognise the scene as it is building and stop it. It will immediately try to re-establish itself as a train of thought but just stop it as soon as it starts. No good can ever come out of it because we are planning a negative future ahead and more importantly, we are not living in the moment, we are not living our life now in the present. This moment is indeed a present and worthy of being lived. **If we let go of the scenario, we meet this person again with no agenda**. It's a fresh start and how we behave will determine our inner state of being and how we present ourselves to the world.

Letting go of scenarios is a very important step in living our life in the now. It is something to really work on consciously. Let the good scenarios form and store them with good intent but let them go too. Enjoy the journey of life that leads up to carrying them out and not just the act itself.

In amongst our thoughts, actions, experiences and the act of being is one of our most important and natural assets, and that is our feelings.

We all know how important feelings are to us. They are constantly present in some form or other and appear naturally as we live our lives. They come from deep within our being and we can't control when and how they will appear. We just feel them. Our senses trigger them and depending on what our senses are telling us depends on which feeling appears first. We can't pre-plan the time and place they will appear because they can only occur in the present moment as that moment is happening. **Feelings are the greatest indicator of what is happening within our core being. How we feel about a feeling is how we will think about it and how we will act upon it.**

There are two extremities at play here, fear and Love. Everyone knows this, it is nothing new, but if we start to pay more attention to it, we can see which camp our thoughts and actions emanate from. We need to become aware of paying attention to it. Paying attention to it means we are becoming *aware* of which we choose. I'm sorry but we are back with Bad wolf and Good wolf again, but the analogy serves an easily understood concept.

I'm not a phycologist and can't delve in to our two primal instincts but every time we act upon our feelings it is from one camp or the other. If we see a runaway car coming towards us, we feel the fear of death and move out of the way to survive. Likewise, but in the other camp, if we are in the right situation we can suddenly feel our hearts open and the feeling of love that is released. These feelings are so opposite that it is easy to feel the difference and to know the difference. It's when the lines get blurred that we can struggle. If they are less extreme in polarity we might not give them too much thought, but they are still there and influencing how we think and act. It can catch us out at any moment and it will. We just keep on keeping on.

A feeling can trigger a thought and a thought can trigger a feeling. The order changes all the time but they are inextricably linked. If we are out in the sun and we are *feeling* too warm, we *think* about it and move in to shade. If we are *thinking* of a friend who has just bought a new car and we are resentful it brings up the *feeling* of envy. **Feelings are something we experience on a personal level and can't be passed on to anyone else unless it is a shared experience**. If I told you that I loved my Mother, I couldn't pass that feeling on to you. I could write page after page telling you why, and you would know from what I have written that I do love my Mother, but you wouldn't *feel* that I do. The same situation experienced by two people can trigger different feelings. If I were about to jump off a bridge attached to a Bungee rope, I would certainly be feeling fear whilst you might be shouting "Yippee" as you jumped off the bridge filled with excitement! **We must trust our feelings because they come from deep within and are telling us how our life is in any particular moment.** It is sometimes not a wise choice to ignore them.

We are constantly being asked "how do we feel about something" and we in turn ask it of others. How we feel about something is how we think and re-act about it unless we take time to pause and act instead of re-act. It's very similar to how we deal with thoughts. If we are feeling resentful it is coming from envy and from the Bad wolf. We are fearful of "not having" and that feeling stirs up thoughts about what we are feeling. Those thoughts often result in a negative reaction which in turn can only produce a negative outcome. We do it unconsciously, **we do it without thinking**, but we do re-act to it consciously. We know we are saying or doing what we shouldn't be. We know it, but we can't stop it, the play has to be acted out. *Unless we don't write the play of course*. Unless we choose to accept we are feeling envious and stop the scenario continuing. If we are aware of how we are behaving, we have a *choice* to carry on or stop it. We can choose to let those feelings go for they are *our* feelings and not of those who we are resentful of. We don't need the permission of the other party to let our own feelings go. **It is obvious, and yet we choose to ignore our inner being that only wants peace for us, and we carry on and create turmoil.** We created the turmoil. Nobody else is responsible. We chose to act out the play and the critics have given us a bad review.

I keep saying this, but there is nothing new in this book, we have all read or heard these words before. It comes down to individual choice if and when we decide we want to live in our life and not be separate to it. A life we take responsibility for, make wiser choices by thinking and acting better, and ultimately making peace with ourselves. Not everyone is fighting an inner battle. I have friends that have no need of this book and I have other friends who desperately need to read it. That's not a judgement but an observation. ***There is a difference***. Judgement comes with an attachment to it, **observation has no such attachment**, it is what it is. It is an acceptance of what is.

CHAPTER FOURTEEN.

Attachment and detachment are once again opposites. If we have a *feeling* about something and we attach a *thought* to it then it becomes an *emotion.*

If we feel anger and we attach a thought to it of why we feel anger and what made us feel anger, we are *creating an emotion.* We are creating another scenario and a play to act out. It develops very quickly from within and usually comes out as an outburst. It is a scene we have written very quickly, subconsciously, *and without thought as to the consequences* and it must be acted out. We open our mouths and our voice gives it the vehicle with which to expend its energy. It is as if we can't stop ourselves and it comes out in full force until the emotion is expelled from our bodies. **It is poisonous to our body and the body wants rid of it and by doing so we expel the negative energy out from within *and in to our lives*.** It is *who we have chosen to be in that moment*. We have allowed the Bad wolf to have a say again and this time we have allowed his fangs to be exposed. Feelings, thoughts and emotions all build so quickly that it is very hard to be in the moment and stop them. *It takes time and a great deal of effort.* We do it one step at a time. There is no other way and it feels like an uphill battle but the very first time we feel anger, *observe* it as anger, and *choose* not to attach anything to it, is a huge step on the pathway to peace and self-mastery. Mastering it just once out of a hundred, is a step made in the right direction. Most of us don't become healed overnight, we must work towards it.

I don't need to remind anyone of all the feelings that emanate from the fear camp, but anger, resentment, jealousy and self-pity are some of the main ones. Some are easier to deal with than others, but some are so ingrained in to our lives that we feel they are a part of us. We *think* that is just how we are but what has happened is that they have attached themselves to us and become a *part of us* when they should be *apart from us*.

If we are heading out to an appointment and a road accident ahead causes us to be in a tailback, there is nothing we can do about it. If it is not possible to divert we must wait until it is safe to proceed. There is no point screaming that we are going to be late. There is no point in screaming at the car in front or banging our fist on the dashboard. No amount of anger or stress can move the car in front until we can all move. It is what it is, and it is better to *accept the situation and live with it.* That is, **live whilst we are in that traffic jam.** We are angry because we are going to be late and our life can only begin when we get *there.* That magical place *there* when life will begin again! We have a life whilst we are sitting there waiting, *don't waste it.* Is there any point in becoming angry? There is only one answer to that question isn't there? If we *accept the situation* our inner being is at peace and we arrive late for the appointment but in a calm and controlled way without the self-inflicted drama. *When I read these words back, I am aware of how I used to behave.* It was always somebody else's fault, but it was a lack of acceptance of my own part in the situation and the choice I had to be either angry or at peace.

Anger can't be suppressed, it must be dealt with at source because otherwise we are holding it within us. If we are involved in an argument and we are in turmoil trying to hold it back, it may appear that we are in control because we didn't let it out in to our lives. To some degree this is correct but if anger is suppressed it will find a way out at some point. It might not be with the person we are arguing with, but it could be the next person, shop-keeper or relative we meet. We need to work at recognising it rising within us and making the instant decision **not to suppress it, but to *let it go***. If we don't allow it to take hold of us it cannot form in to anything significant that needs to be suppressed. Letting it go means that it is no longer within us and won't fester and grow until it makes us take notice, because it will do just that. I know that is not easy to do under pressure but sometimes just a very firm *NO* to ourselves can jolt us in to dealing with it. It just gives us that pause within to *become aware* that we have a choice to make. To choose anger or not choose anger.

We all say and do things we regret. Sometimes the regret is instantaneous and sometimes it comes much later, *but it does come*. If we can just very slowly and surely make an effort to stop letting our emotions be in control of us, we remove the need for regret. Most of us regret the moment instantly, and yet we carry it around with us for some time and we know we could have done better. That thought that we *could have done better* is all the encouragement we need to *try* and do better the next time. We must be gentle with ourselves, they say Rome wasn't built in a day, but I can't vouch for that because I wasn't there! Not that I am aware of anyway.

We are a complex being and we have all our thoughts, feelings, emotions and actions all happening at the same time and it is sometimes difficult in the storm to see that calm will eventually come. Staying upright in the storm is sometimes not easy but if we always look to come from the bigger part of ourselves, we learn to ride the storm and not endure it. At any given moment we are a person living a life and as we live from moment to moment, we have a choice of which part of us to come from. We have the freedom to choose. We always have that choice. Even in adversity we can always choose the better option. It's not easy, I used to hide in the storm and scream *why are you doing this to me*, but nobody seemed to hear. When I learned to stand up again, I found that it was better to keep walking than to hide because eventually I walked out of the storm.

Love is a powerful word. Those four letters express a word and a world that contains everything there is in life. Love cannot live in fear for it is fearless. It knows no boundaries of race, religion, status or circumstance. It enters everywhere freely and without invitation or restriction. Love cannot and will not be denied. When it comes as true love, we feel it in every cell of our body as it embraces us. It comes in many forms, as in the love of a friend, our animals and of our partner or children, but in whatever form love comes it enhances our being.

When we come from the Love within us, the expression of it is harmonious. It expresses itself through love itself, and we experience it in so many ways that are natural to us. As a child we look to our parents to not only receive love, but to give love back, for it is normal to us as we have not yet attached limits. It is without restriction and life has not yet diluted our experience of it. As we grow older it seems that love has conditions attached to it, but it is still our *natural and instinctive* nature to act out of love. If we see an old lady stumble to the ground, we instantly act through compassion to help her to her feet. We didn't have to make a decision about it. We acted instinctively without thinking and without attaching thoughts to it because it is our *natural instinct* to help others in need. It comes from within and without censorship and expresses who we are in that moment. Without thinking, and in a very natural way, we have decided who we are, and it came from a place that is love. Love is our natural state of being when we peel away everything else that masks it.

Love cannot live in fear, but fear can live in love until we accept love unconditionally. That is *without any conditions attached*. Love is simply love, and in its purest form is all that there is. It contains *everything* and all who embrace it unconditionally see that nothing can diminish it. It will not falter, it will not fail, and in its purest form it is stronger than any man, woman or nation. It has the power to change us, and the world we inhabit would be healed overnight if only every being embraced it fully. *It is that simple*. The Universe makes it simple for us, but we choose to complicate it by adding attachments. If we all pulled together for the love of each other and for the love of our planet there would be nothing *but* love in our lives. Unconditional love unites, it does not separate. It chooses everyone and everything in its path and is the only code of conduct we need to live by. If we live through love, we can't hurt anyone for we hurt ourselves. Unconditional love is given to us by our Creator. We are loved so much that we are free to live our lives freely for if it were not that way it would not be unconditional love.

Conditional love is a very poor imitation of pure love. Conditional love is a fertile place for fear to breed. There is a very fine line between love and hate and it is fear that straddles that line. We cross that line very quickly if we attach conditions to love. We love our partner if they love us back and do it within the boundaries we have set. If they cross that boundary our love can instantly turn to hate. *Is that really love*? Our love is conditional on condition that it is restricted and moulded in to our version of love? We forbid the loving of anyone else as if that very command can stop it. Conditional love contains so much fear that it can very easily change in to the fear of love. If we are in a relationship that uses love as a means of controlling the other partner, it is like owning an animal that must be chained up for it to remain with us. It is better to let go of the fear of losing love and remove the chains. In doing so we conquer fear *through love* of that person and by setting them free we just might find that once the chains are removed there was no need for them in the first place.

CHAPTER FIFTEEN.

I want to try and explain what I mean by connecting with our Higher Self. I want to try to put it in to words and a description, that can hopefully be understood. I have read so many books where it is brought up almost as if the person is talking to another person as casually as talking to their partner. It leaves the reader feeling separated from the idea because it seems to be something that the person "just does" and the mechanics of it feel way beyond us. It seems beyond our grasp and normality because it seems so surreal and almost like a fairy-tale in the way it is put across. It can also come across that they are special in some way, and must be, because it doesn't happen to us. It does happen to us. We are just not aware of it yet. **It happens much more frequently than we are _aware_ of and recognising it just takes a little time of careful and quiet practice.**

I will explain a "conversation" I had with my Higher Self that prompted me to write this chapter but first I must lay the foundation that led to my "conversation".

I had made the commitment to myself that I wanted to change and that I wanted to fill the void that was inside of me. My physical life was fine, but I was empty inside. The piece of me that was missing prompted me to search for the answers.

I made the decision to change but I also made the decision to carry on writing this book which I had previously started and stopped over a long period of time. I was making progress in both my spiritual growth and the writing of this book, but after the initial flood of euphoria that carried me with it, came the doubts. I am not an author, I am not an intellectual being with high intellect, I am just an ordinary guy. Why would anyone want to read a book from me? It was and is, a very fair question to ask myself and the doubts increased. One evening I was alone and sitting quietly in my chair. I was thinking about this book and worrying about the doubts that I had. I seemed to let the thoughts ebb away and I became a little less troubled but still no insights came.

I was about to stand up to go to bed when I found myself asking a question in my head to God, who I call Father. I was about to ask, "Do I have to write this book?" but as I formed the word "I", I suddenly stopped the thought and changed it to *We*. I changed the question to "Do *we* have to write this book?" As soon as I voiced it in thought *I was given an instant answer*. There was a flash of light and the room lit up like the flash from a camera and the television satellite box flickered briefly on and then off. It was briefly but it happened at the exact moment I asked my question. I am aware enough to know it was no coincidence. It was a very clear sign and a very clear answer to my question. It removed the doubts and I carried on writing with renewed vigour.

A few days later I was driving in to Aberdeen. The radio was on in the car and a song came on from the band Runrig. They have been a favourite band of mine for over 40 years and they are very big in Scotland, but their records are seldom played on mainstream radio. They had just played their final show after 45 years and the announcer, Ken Bruce, was playing "The Last Dance". I was singing and rocking away to the track and thoroughly enjoying myself when a "thought" came through over the top of the track. It came through loud and clear but in a "thought" and it was this: *"You do know this book is going to change your life* don't *you? Are you ready for it?"* I instantly replied but in my own voice and out loud *"We are in this together, so are you ready for it?!"* It was a very emotional moment for me for it was almost saying the book *would* be completed and my life would change. It was another confirmation that I must keep writing. I didn't know how at the time it would change my life and I didn't care how I just knew that a change would take place and that it would be for the better.

That is the foundation for my conversation with myself, so I will fast forward to that.

I was lying in bed and thinking about the writing I had done that day. Lynn was away for the week with her friends on holiday and I was home alone with Becky. I had known this week was approaching and I had set it aside to get stuck in to the book. Now the week was upon me and I was feeling the pressure of writing. I had just finished Chapter Fourteen which you have just read, but at that point I had ended with the words "There is a difference" and I had saved it and left it at that. It was as if the answer to that final statement was left hanging in mid-air.

 Whilst lying there in bed the doubts came once again. I had just written about Feelings and as I had closed the chapter, I had realised I had now to write about Emotions. It all felt very heavy and beyond me. Once again, the Bad wolf was whispering in to my ear "who did I think I was?" and "who would want to read a book written by *you*?" Once again it begged the question "Well, who would?" and the doubts circled again. As I laid there, I started to remember the sign I had been given. It was a very real answer at the time and it still felt it now. I pondered on it and then remembered the "thought" that came in over the car radio and once again I was encouraged by it to keep on writing.

I was thinking how I had left the last chapter with an almost unanswered question and I was also thinking of how on earth I would follow it with emotions when *my Higher Self stepped in.* It stepped in through "thought". I started to be *aware* of my thoughts because they seemed to come in to my mind just a little louder than a normal thought. It was only just noticeably so, but the thought had a depth to it that is hard to explain. It was so subtle, but it was like asking, was I really feeling and hearing that difference? It was *my* "thoughts", but it felt like I wasn't having to "think" them, they were just appearing like a normal thought but with a subtle sheen to them but also, they were answering my doubts with substance to write about. I will repeat the last few sentences of Chapter Fifteen in normal type, so you can see where I left off, and then in bold I will add text to show the answer I received.

"Not everyone is fighting an inner battle. I have friends who have no need for this book and I have other friends who desperately need to read it. That is not a judgement but an observation. There is a difference. **Judgement comes with an attachment to it, observation has no such attachment, it is what it is. It is an acceptance of what is."**

The words in bold were the very subtle thoughts given to me by my Higher Self. They were barely distinguishable from my "own" thoughts, but the content was more profound. They were coming from a deeper place within me. It answered the "difference" question and finished the chapter. I suddenly felt that I wasn't alone in all of this again and I began to relax away from the pressure.

I lay thinking, along the lines of, *"Look, if this book is only meant to help me, then it is doing its job, it is healing me, but if the book is to help others, then it needs to be written by someone better than a gasfitter. It needs the magic putting in to it if it is to touch others and only you can do that. So, here's the deal, I will be your messenger and I will write down what you give me and then the magic will appear. I will be the best scribe you could ever have, and I will see the book through, but you can be the author."* Phew, the pressure was off and very nicely deflected too!

I started to relax even more as I lay there and was perhaps feeling a little smug at my deflection, but then I started to think how *we* would follow Feelings with Emotions when that subtle awareness of thought started again. A very gentle increase in volume and depth but again with words that were answers. This is what I heard **"Emotions are just feelings with a thought attached to them. If we are to control our emotions, we must learn attachment and detachment of our thoughts"**

Once again, I have highlighted in bold what my Higher Self passed on to me through a very subtle but different timbre in the thoughts I was hearing. It was a very natural process and just felt normal as it was happening because it just felt like me. It was me but it was the *real* me.

It gave me the start of the next chapter and a way of seamlessly writing from one subject to another. It looked like I was back in the saddle again but this time with a deeper sense of purpose and an ever-increasing trust that this is meant to be.

So, who or what, is our Higher Self?

It is the gateway to who we really are as a being on this earth. It is our Soul and was given to us as we entered our physical body. It is the gift of life. It remains within our Being as we walk this life and only leaves when we lay our body down. As it leaves it takes who *we really are* with it. Our Spirit becomes free of physical limitations and it now has new experiences of its soul journey. It contains all we know about ourselves and the Universe around us. It is such a powerful and life changing part of us and yet we mostly deny or ignore its existence.

Everyone reading this has heard of the Soul. *Everyone*. It's in our everyday language but we do not see past the word. We say, "Hey man…this music has soul!" Or "oh she's such a gentle soul" or even "He's an old soul" but although it is a nice enhancement to the music or person it isn't seen beyond that. If music has soul, then what is it about that music? It is simply because it has touched us. Where has it touched us? We delight in the rhythm and the vibration of the music and our ears enjoy the sensation but where does it *touch* us? It touches our inner being, the soul. That's where we feel it. Whenever something really moves us and our bodies tremble with delight, it is our soul that causes the ripple yet after the sensation has gone it is ignored again. We ignore our soul because we can't see it when we look in the mirror, we only feel it on the rare occasions when we can't deny "something" happened, and it is this nice "myth" we have heard about. It's a very comforting myth because it is nice to think we have something within us that is attached to something greater but for most of us it stays locked away. It seems we only notice it when the soul does the prodding and not when *we* choose to, and yet, *it is us that is holding the key*, and when the time is right, we can unlock the door to our inner

Being and experience the soul. There is no way of knowing what it will take for us to use that key, but when that day comes, and the lock is turned, it opens a whole new world we have only dreamt about. A world that is so real we can hardly believe how simple it was to access it. It just takes a decision and whatever makes us decide, is a truly great moment, even if it is in the middle of adversity.

This book is about walking in harmony through life with ourselves and our surroundings. It is not about a destination but a way of enjoying the journey. Throughout my life I have been shown the other world. I have crossed over that invisible line and experienced the other side. It has at times brought me to my knees with the wonderment of it all but also it has brought me to my knees with how unworthy I was of seeing it. It has sometimes even been hard saying hello to my neighbour after such an experience because it was hard to function on a daily level.

I think half of us look outside of ourselves for our answers and we see the other half appearing to have what we are looking for. This may or may not be true. If we truly want our *own* answers, that is, answers to the Self, we must look within. For my part, I was seeing and experiencing some of the answers that seemed to be outside of myself. Experiences that seemed to be outside of me and I wanted more. ***I wanted more, yet I couldn't honour what I had already been given.*** I had been crying out for more, for proof, and it was a genuine cry from the heart which the soul was answering, but immediately I was given what I asked for, I couldn't accept it fully. I could not accept it fully because I was in denial. I could accept the answers, but I could not accept *me*. It wasn't the acceptance of me "the privileged" or me "the special one" or any other aggrandisement you want to add. I am just an ordinary person and just the same as any other person walking this earth and yet I didn't feel like it. I felt lesser than. I have been given such knowledge and yet I couldn't even accept myself as rising to the level of ordinary or whatever ordinary is. That is why I felt different. **Please don't read different as saying better. I wrote the word different and not better**. I felt like I was walking in parallel to my life. I had one life that looked outwardly that was given answers and one that walked beside but couldn't honour the answers. *It was the distance between the two that was the void I had to fill.* The void was so vast and so empty that it was causing me pain and unrest. I had to bring both paths together to create one path. It is the pathway to within and leads to peace. It is also the road less travelled, but it is the only way I could walk in harmony with myself and to accept who I am. I am Brian. No more and no less. When I made the decision to turn the key I stepped in to my life.

After weeks and months of consciously trying to make peace with myself I finally stepped in to my own skin. I finally honoured myself and my Spirit as One being. It has taken me a lifetime, but I am finally *living* in my own life. I am trusting my inner voice and the guidance I receive from myself, that is, My Self.

CHAPTER SIXTEEN.

When we talk about guidance from within, we are really speaking about following our own advice.

The guidance is coming from our Self but from the part of us that only wants the very best for us. In all of this we are never told what to do. It is not how the Universe works. We have free-will and we can exercise that free-will in any way we choose. If the Higher Self was to say you must do this, then that universal law is broken. We are never told what to do but by connecting with our soul we have a bigger picture of the question we are asking ourselves. It allows us to make perhaps a better decision based on intuition or a knowing what the correct answer is really. We often know the answer before we ask but sometimes voicing it inwardly allows confirmation in part.

The worst thing about this scenario is that we are the last person we go to for meaningful advice! We can accept our own advice to choose the blue shirt over the white one or the brown shoes over the black, but if it is of anything deeply spiritual and especially of the universal truth, we think any meaningful answer must come from somewhere else. It must come from *outside of us* when we already have all the answers we need *within us.* Once we fully accept this concept and accept that our answers are inside of us we can truly journey within. We open the door to our soul that contains all the answers *that are and ever will be.*

The soul can open an outer door to access the Universe and all it contains and then we also start another journey but that is for another book.

If we have a problem or a question to ask and we don't believe in anything like the soul, our inner being, or our higher self, we still start by asking our *self* the question. We still seek an outcome of our problem from our own minds. If we can't come to an answer or conclusion we then turn to friends. Our close friends can listen and help us to see a way though the situation. It gives us another perspective and we may be shown a bigger picture by their guidance. We can take advice, but we must take responsibility for the decision we make. Ultimately it is our choice.

The Higher Self behaves in the exact same way. *It is our very best friend*. It knows us intimately and it knows the best solution for our journey, and so the guidance we receive is only in our best interest. The thoughts that come through are given in the same good intent as our friend, **but they come from a point of knowing**. We are just given a bigger picture and a clearer view of the problem. Thoughts come through in that barely increased volume that ring of the truth and hearing them gives clarity to the situation. It doesn't take away the decision we have to make but it does lend to a sense of making a fully informed decision. That decision can still be very hard to make and sometimes we must make decisions that are for our greater good. It's not all fairy dust, but neither is life.

We also receive guidance in a very natural way through intuition.

If thoughts are the Soul's prompts, then intuition is the soul's voice and expression through feelings. We have all felt that nudge in the pit of our stomach and either gone along with it or ignored it. It is a very natural way for the soul to operate and some people, mostly female, are very in tune with it. We know something without knowing why, we just have a hunch.

Our soul is the very essence of who we really are. Tuning in to the vibrations that emanate from the soul and run through our bodies can take time and practice. It's not easy in a crowded supermarket whilst talking to someone, to slow our thoughts down enough to hear our inner thoughts about the conversation. We simply take what we are hearing at face value and decide how we feel about it at human level. That is our normal state of operation, the human level. We can, however, trust our intuition on how we are feeling about it. It usually prompts us to either go along with what we are feeling, be neutral or benign in what we feel, or be wary of what we are feeling and hearing. This is no slight on the other person. It is simply trusting what our body is telling us whilst the mind is engaged in conversation. I can't tell you how many times I have bought something I thought I really needed, but would later come to regret, simply by ignoring that nudge. The *need of it* overcomes the *need for it* and invariably a few days or weeks later I find myself thinking why did I buy that? We just need to become more in tune with ourselves and it happens just by being *aware* of our *self*. We can still ignore that intuition if we *choose* to, we are not chained by it, but invariably we find our initial intuition was right all along.

The soul doesn't like conflict. It has a deep desire to live in harmony. Our Spirit would much rather reside in a vessel at ease than one at war with itself. Everyone has an inner conflict at some point in their life, but I would hazard a guess that for most of us it is an ongoing one. We just seem to accept it as part of life and **It is until the time we deal with it**. If we talk intimately with our closest friends, we invariably learn that they too are fighting an inner battle. Outwardly we perceive that everything is fine, but it can mask what is really happening within. I have often been surprised to find that not everything in a friend's world is how I thought it was. They are fighting or have been fighting a battle just like the rest of us. Invariably, if they open up to us, we help without judgement because we sense they are sharing their inner sanctum and we treat it with respect. It just seems a natural thing to do to be compassionate. It takes great courage on their part to share at such a deep level and we must treat their trust with respect. If we can show such compassion to others, why do we feel that if we share our own inner thoughts, we don't deserve the same compassion back? We see sharing *our* thoughts as a weakness in ourselves but do not see that in a friend. *Sharing is a strength and not a weakness*. We need to remind ourselves of that sometimes.

Without generalising too much, I think conflict comes in two forms. One is a conflict with life itself. It is the battle outside of us that also affects us inwardly. The daily conflict of employment, marriage, children, housing, food etc. and the real every day issues that come with it. It is a very real conflict and managing what is going on in our life can bring real stress and worry. It is an outward problem that has a very real effect on our inner being. It is hard to be at peace whilst worrying over bills or where we are going to live.

We all have these problems and trying to follow a spiritual path does not remove them. It can bring an inner battle just as fierce as the outer battle. If we are struggling in our physical life as well as our spiritual life it can feel like *nothing* in our world is going the right way for us. It can bring turmoil in to our lives and any sense of peace is lost. The loss of peace usually means the loss of our self. We just feel lost. If we can find that inner peace it will permeate in to our physical lives. Once inner peace is experienced there inevitably comes the desire to maintain it. We may find a *need* to deal with our problems in order to resolve back to that peaceful state. It may just mean tackling something sooner rather than later and that may also stop the problem escalating. When we operate from that place within, we are in our power and it gives us the strength to face things even though we may not like or be able to control the outcome. It gives us the strength and wisdom to accept what is. Some things we cannot change but peace can come with the acceptance of it.

The inner conflict is a very real one. It almost seems like we must deal with the outer problems first before we can even think about taking time to look after our spiritual wellbeing and yet they go hand in hand. Taking care of one helps to take care of the other. I am very aware that my own progress has gone in cycles. At times I have concentrated on my physical life so that I am then free to concentrate on my spiritual life. *It doesn't work that way*. Life requires attention to both at the same time. Finding our inner voice, our soul, allows us to deal with all sides of life *in the moment it is happening*. **There is no separation of our self from our *Self*, there is only unity of Self**. We become a being at One with ourselves and become *present* in our life at every living moment. We are no longer two separate beings that only come together when circumstances permit. We are a unified being who is simply Being. This is *living* life and taking control of it. We begin to choose how we live our life and not live the one that *just happens*.

If we are walking our spiritual path and are feeling conflict within, then take that as progress. Take that as a pat on the back. We are simply being reminded and made *aware* that because we have chosen the inner journey, we must deal with some part of the conflict simply because we are *aware* of it. We are awake, and we feel it within. If we are asleep, we are oblivious to it. It is a wonderful sign that we are on the right path and should be taken as a gentle nudge to resolve at least some part of the conflict. **Our soul does not want to hurt us**. It wants to bring peace within and it is making us aware of what we need to deal with to be at peace. We dismantle the conflict one piece at a time. If we *know* we are carrying a grudge about someone, we are fully *aware* of it. We can choose to keep on carrying it but no good can come of it. We are being poisoned by it. Peace cannot come from the turmoil it causes within. We must choose to let it go. It doesn't matter who or what caused the grudge, but it has manifested within and is eating away at us. Let it go. Be the bigger person. If we do that we are listening to our inner voice and we are beginning to walk in harmony with our Self. How do we climb a mountain? Ok.........I know I'm pushing it now.

It does take great courage to take that first step. We think we know how we operate as a person and although we may wish to change, we know it will take time and willpower so sometimes it can feel easier to remain where we are. It makes us feel comfortable but only for a very short time. If we have the *need* inside to change who we are, we will not live comfortably knowing that we are standing still. Do not fear what we will change in to or what we may have to let go of to change. It happens slowly and naturally. It is not just the mind we are changing it is our whole being and we are becoming who *we really are* and what we once held as a necessity in our life will just fall away without causing us concern. It is only the ego that doesn't want to let go of anything or to undergo any change. We deal with the ego one thought at a time until it no longer has a voice that we choose to listen to.

I stood alone at my own crossroads for a very long time. I knew it was going to be the hardest decision of my life. I knew I would be leaving everything I thought I knew of myself behind and it was unknown territory ahead. I was frightened and yet I knew I couldn't go back from where I had come. There was no life there anymore. I also knew that if I chose to turn left or right it would only be a diversion. The only road remaining was to walk straight ahead. I made the decision to take it and I left my baggage behind.

It turned out to be the best decision I have ever made. I haven't looked back.

CHAPTER SEVENTEEN.

We can't wait for Perfect.

The perfect time, place or situation will never come. The Universe stands back and allows us the grace and time to make our decision. We might not even make it in this lifetime. We alone must make our choice. Once we do make the decision and turn the key to open our inner door it isn't just the gears of the lock that are set in motion. We set the whole Universe in motion for in turning that key a cosmic change takes place and the gears turn throughout the Universe as a new path is created for us. We don't walk it alone. We have never walked alone but now we become aware of it. Each one of us is unique and cherished by the Universe for it needs our completion for itself to be complete. We are that important. *You* are that important.

A lot of decisions to make that inner journey are made through and out of adversity. If that is the case do not feel like you were forced in to it. The pain inside of you allowed your soul to step forward and by loving you intensely it helped *you* to make the decision you were always going to make anyway. Feel proud of yourself and walk forward with grace for you have earned it.

Walk slowly to begin with. Start gently and begin to experience *who you really are*. A good place to start is by observing your thoughts. Just observe how you think and what you think but pay no attention to trivial thoughts. Do not give them a place to rest in your mind, simply allow them to pass through. A silence is being created and from within that silence our inner voice has the chance to be heard.

Do not berate yourself if you find it difficult to stop "thinking", it *will* come through practice. Be patient with yourself and love yourself for the very act of trying.

Try not to create scenarios from your thoughts. *They serve no purpose*. **Thinking about a problem is different to creating a scenario about it**. Try to separate the two. We all need to think about things we need to deal with but don't write a story around them. Just observe and realise which part of the problem is important. Let go of the trivia and deal with the substance.

Try not to let your thoughts spur you in to re-acting to anything. Instead, try to act consciously because that is through choice. If we get angry, we must know that we chose that emotion. Understanding this, *and the acceptance of it*, is a huge step forward. Once we accept that we have chosen to feel anger we quickly decide not to choose it.

Stand firm in your own space. Make it sacred and only allow those you choose to enter it. Your inner sanctum is not an open door that anyone can walk through and you have the right to deny access. **That means from anyone in your life.** We can give outwardly to others of our self, but we must have a sacred space where we can be ourselves without justification to anyone else. Learn to say No without justification. Say it with a smile but be firm. Try not to let words hurt you, for if you allow it, then you have given every person you meet the weapon to destroy you. Merely observe the words, observe how *you* are feeling about them and deal with the ensuing emotions. Let whatever emotion is surfacing leave you and pay it no attention. You are living in *your* moment and *you* are in control. You are becoming your own Master. In becoming our own Master, we understand that we can never be master over anyone else. We simply allow anyone to be who they choose to be in that moment without judgement or the desire to change them. When we see a desire to change coming from within them, we can then step forward and ask, "How can I help you". **In that moment we see ourselves in the other person and we realise we are truly all related as part of the Whole**. There is no hierarchy, no levels of knowledge, no separation, but simply a deep and natural desire to help for in doing so we are experiencing who we really are. We don't teach knowledge, we share it and that makes us equal as both teacher and pupil.

Love everyone. That is tremendously hard to do. If we can't love everyone we interact with we must try and see them as ourselves. Give ourselves course to be reminded that they may inwardly be struggling too. Hear their words, observe their emotions and act with compassion and without passing judgement. **Nobody likes to feel they have been judged over something they are struggling with or a mistake they made**. *We all make mistakes*. If we judge them by their mistakes, it is our attempt to define who they are, and we confine their being and restrict their growth. If we understand them, we set them free, but in our time of understanding we also define who we are. We all have situations in our life that lead to conflict. We don't have to win the argument. We win by taking part and being the best person we have ever been.

We are not on a journey to become a Saint. We just need to become our Self. Do not fear change. Don't worry who you will turn in to and what you may have to leave behind to be that person. Change comes slowly in the same way our hair grows, and it is barely noticeable at first. Those around you may not even notice or acknowledge any change but you will know inside of you a change is taking place. Trust yourself and believe in yourself. The desire to bring about change will make it happen and anything we need to let fall away will fall away naturally. What we once considered important will no longer have that label attached to it. It will just be what it is. It will remain part of our life or it will leave us.

Finally, opening the door to the Kingdom that resides within will change your life. You will experience not only yourself, but life itself in the most enjoyable and peaceful way that was never thought possible. **You will experience who you really are and who you really are is beyond any words I can write.** You are magnificent in all your glory as a human *being* human.

Walk in harmony with your Self and everyone and everything around you for you are a part of it. You are no longer apart from it. You truly belong here.

CHAPTER EIGHTEEN.

I wrote this chapter after I had supposedly finished the book. I took a short break to reflect on what I had written, and I knew that whilst editing I would add or subtract text.

This is perhaps the most important chapter of my own personal journey. In trying to walk in harmony with my *self* I was journeying on the path to self-Mastery. I wanted to take control of my life and *live* my life as it happens. I wanted to be in control of how I lived it so that I was a part of it and not separate to it. I wanted to live my life in awareness of it. The road to self-mastery and taking control of one's life does not assume it is a spiritual path also. That is a personal choice each of us must make on our journey. Seeking the spiritual is where it started for me and so it was a natural choice that I would combine the two. As we journey, we are given insights and signs along the way but sometimes, even if the penny drops instantly, we don't always assimilate it in to our lives immediately. We ponder on it and it creates a pause. It gives us time to think and it also allows the Universe to observe the outcome of our decision. Once we start to actively seek we can assimilate what we are given much quicker and begin to use it in our lives. The journey seems to be quickening and it gives us encouragement to keep on keeping on.

Whilst reflecting on the book and the words it contained something truly wonderful happened. I simply assimilated the book in to my life and became the book. I don't really know how to explain it better than that. I realised that all I had written about I have been putting in to practice **as I wrote it** and with that realisation my next intake of breath introduced me to a new life. It is a life in which I have chosen to be the master of Self. It does not mean I am there yet, it does not mean life has no mistakes anymore it simply means that I have chosen to write my own destiny. I have chosen to steer my own course through life and if I come across rough ground it is of my own making and I take responsibility for it. It means journeying onwards one step, one thought and one action at a time but this time living the journey.

Something extremely personal and important to my journey also came out of realising the book. I have written earlier that when I asked the question should we write this book I received a very clear sign. It was a very simple statement affirming that I should. *It promised nothing in return.* I have also written that over the top of a loud rock song playing on the radio came the thought "*you do know this book will change your life don't you and are you ready for it?*" I simply answered that I was ready for it. **That insight made only one promise in that the book would change my life**. *It has done it in a way far beyond any comprehension I had at the time*. It has changed *Me.* That is what the insight promised, and the promise has been kept. I am changed.

 I hope that in sharing my journey it will help others too. That is a wish that comes from my heart and soul to all of those who may read this book as part of their search for the truth and is beyond any of my wildest dreams. It took courage to cast my stone in to the pond and I have no means of knowing how far the ripples will go and who they may touch. It has been worth it for my journey has now become a healing one and is making me whole and I give thanks to all those living and in spirit who have held my hand until I could stand up alone.

Those insights that were given whilst I was struggling to validate the book served two very different purposes. They gave me the strength and courage to keep on writing, and that there was a reason for this book. That reason has now become abundantly clear to me.

Those insights also gave the ego another chance to keep a hold of me. I naturally want to have the book published to help others in the same way that it was helping me as I wrote it. I started to believe that perhaps I could eke out a living as an author and the *desire and need* to have it published took over. I am fully aware that there is nothing wrong with wanting to be successful in life and working towards achieving that goal. I still want this book to be published and for all the right reasons and I will actively seek it.

However, the *desire* and *need* to have it published has left me.

I was given this book freely by the Universe. I have carried out my part and I have seen it to completion. I now give it back to the Universe as my gift and I give it freely and without condition.

I am Brian.

I am a part of the Whole and I belong here.

In Closing......

When I was a young child we lived in a very small house in Bradford. It was just one room downstairs and two small bedrooms upstairs. There was no kitchen or bathroom. The only heat we had was from a single coal fire, but oh how magical that fire was to me! It had to be lit every day and it needed kindling and newspaper to get it going. Mum and Dad worked all day, so I would come home from school and let myself in. I was far too young to wield an axe, but I would head down in to the cellar and chop kindling from the old wood Dad would collect from building sites. Soon I was trusted to light the fire and what a thrill that was! I would chop my kindling and watch the pile grow and grow with an ever-increasing smile on my face. It wasn't work for me, it was sheer joy and the freedom of being in my own space and creating something out of it. Life was bliss and I was smiling.

Somewhere along the way life got involved and yet the "wood still had to be chopped" but it became one of life's chores. I lost my smile.

I'm back chopping my wood. We have a woodburning stove and it needs kindling. My pile of kindling grows with every stick I cut, and every stick brings joy. I belong on this earth and I am smiling again.

Printed in Great Britain
by Amazon